To Patrick!
Best wishes—
Virginia Snyder
6-22-11

... AND JUSTICE FOR ALL

The Improbable Story of Virginia Snyder,
Investigative Reporter and Private Investigator

By
Virginia Artrip Snyder
and
Sandra Sobel Reddemann

iUniverse, Inc.
New York   Bloomington

And Justice For All
The Improbable Story of Virginia Snyder,
Investigative Reporter and Private Investigator

iUniverse books may be ordered through booksellers or by contacting:

iUniverse
1663 Liberty Drive
Bloomington, IN 47403
www.iuniverse.com
1-800-Authors (1-800-288-4677)

ISBN: 978-0-595-45076-3 (pbk)
ISBN: 978-0-595-71239-7 (cloth)
ISBN: 978-0-595-89387-4 (ebk)

Printed in the United States of America

CONTENTS

PREFACE

I look like thousands of other elderly women in South Florida: short, plump, white-haired, and spectacled. These looks have served me well. I was a private investigator for twenty-two years, and my grandmotherly appearance got me into all sorts of places. Just about anyone would talk to me. I was also the inspiration for Jessica Fletcher in *Murder She Wrote*, the hit television show on CBS during the 1980s.

This book is about me: How I survived an abusive childhood to become a determined private investigator. How a shy and miserable girl matured into a woman who didn't fear confrontation with local government officials, police departments, or state prosecutors in order to help victims of injustice. Indeed, I became known for my compassion and thoroughness. Word spread that if you were innocent of a crime, there was a good chance that I might find evidence to help you. If you were not, you should not hire me, because I might find evidence to put you away!

In addition to being a private investigator, I am also a poet. I began writing poetry as an emotional outlet during my difficult childhood. Poetry has been my friend. It has inspired me, consoled me, strengthened me, and helped me to understand myself. It has also helped me to laugh at myself. I share some of my poems throughout the book to add depth to the narrative.

Throughout my life, I have probed more than one hundred homicides, including fifteen death-row cases, whereby I helped save six men from execution. My cases have included a retired teacher whose dismembered body was hidden in a trunk; a pedophile who killed a sixteen-year-old and got away with murder because he was an informer for the police department; an attorney who held one of his elderly wards hostage; and a Cuban fry cook, Luis Diaz, who was unjustly convicted and imprisoned as a serial rapist for twenty-six years. But ... *And Justice For All* is more than individual cases; it is also about the corruption and callousness of many officials who were and are major players in our justice system.

This book is about my searching for justice in Florida, but based on my extensive reading and experience, I believe that circumstances are similar elsewhere in our country. This story is about my successes, as in the Louis Diaz case, and about my continuing challenges, those cases I have not resolved to my satisfaction. I do not believe in the concept of failure because, even as a child, it has never been in my nature to quit. I have fought city hall and won. I know what one person can do to challenge the system.

ACKNOWLEDGMENTS

I owe so much to my beloved husband, Ross, who has encouraged and supported me in everything I have attempted to do since we met in 1953.

In addition, our nephew Wayne Campbell (our "son") has been an invaluable partner since he joined our agency thirty years ago. I always knew I could trust him completely to do the best job possible.

Equal thanks go to Sandy Reddemann, my dear friend and coauthor. This book would not have been written without her. Her ability to organize the material I had already written, rewrite, write from my notes, and edit the whole shebang was incredible. She has my undying thanks for enabling me to tell my story.

Finally, I want to thank all of my other friends and relatives who have believed in me over the years.

Sandra Reddemann writes:

I want to acknowledge my good luck in meeting Virginia Snyder, one of the great women of our times. Until I met Virginia, people like her who have changed society were basically in history books or the biography section of the public library. Now I have the privilege of knowing and writing about a woman who overcame great odds to help her fellow men and women. As a result, I am a changed person, one who will now stand up more firmly for a cause. Thank you, Virginia, for inspiring me. I also want to thank my husband, Jim, for his loving support. Ditto to my children, Beth Brown and Rabbi Andrew Karsh and to my grandchildren for their encouragement. I am also grateful to friends who helped: Selma Cappon and Aileen Frumpkin for their editing skills, Michael Leibowitz and Charles Rhodes for their computer skills.

The Great Divide

I was almost ready to quit
When my personality split.
But now I just love it.
There's twice as much of it;
In fact it has doubled my wit.

HUMBLE
BEGINNINGS

Mama and Daddy were married February 17, 1917, in Richwood, West Virginia, where Daddy owned a general store. They left Richwood for Winchester, Virginia, when Daddy's own father moved to Winchester. Daddy was now a farmer. However, owning a general store had not prepared him for growing food and raising stock. As a result, we were poor, even before the Great Depression. A growing family did not help matters. I was born November 27, 1920, the oldest of six children.

My memories of growing up center on hard work in the fields from the time my siblings and I were big enough to help plant and pick vegetables. I remember how my hands would freeze in the winter when we washed the root vegetables and tied them in bundles to sell to the local store. Many days, Daddy had to hunt squirrels and rabbits for our dinner table, and I had to hold the small creatures while Daddy skinned them. I was sickened by all of the blood.

More importantly, I remember unhappiness in my early years, because Daddy was often cruel to me. When I was seven, he hit me on the head with an ear of corn. I remember the dried corn grains raining down over my face, but I do not remember why he was so angry. Not long after that incident, he hit me on the head with a hammer; to this day, I do not know what made him so angry.

My mother's reaction to this abuse was to weakly plead, "Frank, stop." When he interrupted with an angry "Shut up," she backed off. I never remember her coming near me at those times.

As the eldest child, I had the responsibility of caring for the younger children. It was my fault if they got into trouble or misbehaved. For instance, if they fought over a toy, Daddy gave me a whipping and threw away the toy. One time, I was carrying one of my baby brothers on my hip and dropped him. Actually, he wiggled so much that he slipped out of my grasp, ending up on the floor. Daddy, who was nearby, landed a good kick on my hip while in his stocking feet. I heard a crack and later overheard him telling Mama that he thought he had broken his toe.

There is no doubt about the fact that Daddy was responsible for most of my unhappiness. He was not only abusive physically but also verbally. He was always telling me, "You aren't going to amount to anything. You aren't worth shit, and you're going to end up in reform school." In fact, his threats to send me to reform school started to sound good—better than living at home. Without the abuse I was forced to endure, my life would have been uncomplicated and content.

When I was eight years old, something occurred that brought about a significant change in my life. Daddy said to me, "I'm going into town, and I want you to feed that sick cow while I'm gone. Get your nose out of that book, mix the medicine the vet gave me with some feed, and give it to her."

"I'll do it," I promised, still reading.

As Daddy drove away, I decided I had better take care of the cow right then, or else I might get too absorbed in my book. I went to the barn, mixed the feed and medicine, and watched as the cow ate the mixture, licking the sides of the bucket to get it all. Then I went back to my book.

When Daddy returned, I was sitting in the same spot with the same book. "Did you feed the cow?" he asked.

"Yes, I fed her," I replied without looking up.

"I'm going out to see." He returned in a few minutes with anger on his face.

"You lied to me; there isn't a speck of feed in the bucket.

"She ate it all," I explained.

"You're lying," he shouted. "I'll teach you to lie to me!" He grabbed a good-sized switch and confronted me again.

"You didn't feed that cow, did you?"

"I did."

Whack! "Did you?"

"I did."

Whack! "Did you?"

"I did."

Mama came into the room as Daddy continued to beat me and pleaded with him to stop. "Frank, you'll kill the child!" The harshness of her voice encouraged me to think that this time she would help.

"Get back and shut up," he snarled.

Mama cowered in fear, crying hysterically as he continued to whip me, getting a second switch when the first one broke.

I was determined that he was not going to make me lie and just as determined that I would not cry. Finally, when the second switch broke, he stomped out of the house, slamming the door behind him. Only then did I cry. It hurt so bad, I couldn't help it.

Mama counted forty-two welts on my body, some of them bloody. After she put salve on them, I went outside. "I wish he would die; I wish he would die," I muttered.

Then I looked defiantly at each cloud, fully expecting a lightening bolt to strike me dead. I wondered which cloud it would come from. Having attended fundamentalist Sunday schools since I could remember, I knew that I would be struck dead. We were taught that God sees and knows everything and punishes a man who curses his brother. Nothing happened. I decided that there must not be a God. And so it was that I became an atheist.

I reasoned that if God did not exist, the dire predictions about what would happen to me if I were not good weren't true—nor were the warnings about what would happen to sinners, nor was all the rest of my religious instruction. I'll admit that I was not a total disbeliever at that point. For a few years, I harbored some leftover fears that surfaced once in a while, but I had a wonderful sense of freedom that I had never felt before. I could think whatever I wanted—and nobody, not even God (if there was one), could stop me!

Despite my new revelation, when I was about nine years old, my parents had me baptized. The minister dipped me backward three times in the creek. The water was very cold, and I thought I would drown. The baptism did not stop me from questioning. Years later, after studying all the great religions and philosophy and reasoning things out for myself, I decided that the Golden Rule is all we need to live by.

Despite my newfound freedom from fears about God, I was still miserable as a result of Daddy's abuse, and I began to have nightmares. I would see lions and tigers coming at me and would wake up screaming.

I felt trapped. I dreaded going to bed. Then something beautiful happened.

One night, when I was trying very hard to stay awake, I felt myself float out of bed, out of my room, down the stairs, and out into the night. I floated above the countryside, almost as if I were wearing seven-league boots. After a while, I floated back home, back to my room and bed. What a wonderful experience! What a peaceful feeling! It was something out of a fairy tale. I did not fight going to bed after that, because I wanted to repeat that same out-of-this-world experience. It happened again, but only a few times. Nevertheless, it was enough to cure me of my fear of nightmares and perhaps save my sanity.

But things would soon change for me. The summer before seventh grade, my Grandfather Artrip visited us and took me back to Richwood, West Virginia, for a visit. (Although he originally moved to Winchester with my father in 1921, he stayed only a few years and then returned to Richwood.) Richwood is in the mountains, along a river that was near my grandfather's house. I loved to go to that river and climb up on a huge boulder. I would lie there and daydream for hours.

Summer ended, but I was not taken home for two more months, even though school was already in session. I never knew why I could not go home in time for school; but instead of getting caught up at school when I did return, I read books from the library. I had learned that reading was my salvation. No matter what was wrong, I could forget everything if I had a book to read. That school year I read over seventy books, but I did no homework in any of my classes, so I failed seventh grade. My problems in school only got worse.

During my second year in the seventh grade, I began to have jerky movements, nervous tics, and poor coordination. By the time I entered eighth grade, these symptoms worsened. I would also drop things and fall. Finally, in the middle of the school year, I had to drop out. The school nurse urged Daddy to take me to a specialist on Huntington's disease. Instead, Daddy took me to Dr. C. R. Anderson, our family doctor, who had delivered my first three siblings and me. Dr. Anderson was a blunt man and used strong language; however, he was a concerned and caring doctor who knew his patients, their families, their lifestyles, and their finances—everything about them. After listening to the description of my symptoms and asking a few questions, he turned to Daddy.

4

"There isn't a damn thing wrong with this child, Frank, except that you're beating the hell out of her."

Without a word, Daddy grabbed me by the arm and dragged me out of the office. Back home, he stormed at Mama, "Don't ever go to him for anything."

Mama did not dare disobey him, so Dr. L. M. Allen delivered her last two children.

About this time, an elderly couple who had been missionaries in South America retired and moved to Winchester. After my parents met the Connerleys, Mama told them about my illness and said that I had been forced to drop out of school. They quickly figured out the situation and how to get around Daddy in order to help me. As soon as the Connerleys got the chance, they told Daddy that they were lonely and wondered if he would allow me to stay with them while I was not in school. Daddy felt sorry for them. "If they want her to keep them company, it's all right with me."

The next three months with Mamita and Popita were heaven. They let me read as much as I wanted and let me listen to classical music. They treated me with kindness and taught me what love means. They taught me by example. When Popita would go out, Mamita would first make sure that he had a warm scarf around his neck. She would tuck it in, then stand on tiptoe to kiss his cheek. His happy smile and her solicitous gesture were something entirely new to me.

I had never seen my parents kiss each other or demonstrate, in any way, that they loved or even liked one another. I was amazed. The tenderness between Mamita and Popita made such an everlasting impression on me that it taught me to express my love naturally and spontaneously. I am forever grateful.

After three months, my condition had improved so much that I was able to go back to school. I studied very hard and made up the missed work. I was ready to go into ninth grade.

I Remember

There were not many good times
In life when I was small.
Since there are so very few,
They're easy to recall.

Memories are as sharp and clear
As anything could be.
Close my eyes and they are there,
So much a part of me.

Dewdrops dripping from a leaf,
Small pebbles in a stream,
Deep, dark woods in which to hide,
A secret place to dream.
To find a four-leaf clover
Was always such a thrill. To catch a little minnow,
To climb a little hill.

But then there were the beatings—
I think of them as well.
Although there were some good times,
My early years were hell.

HITCHING A RIDE
WITH THE GILPINS

When I was eight years old, I started going to school. Until that time, a neighbor who homeschooled her son also taught me, but when my younger sister was ready for first grade and I was ready for third, we were allowed to walk to our schoolhouse. There were no school buses. In winter we froze. Part of the nearly three-mile trek was a windswept road that seemed to have no end. There was only one tree and one house on this part of our journey. We had been told not to stop at the house, because they had a son who "was not all there," according to Daddy. Sometimes, however, when the weather was really bad, we did stop to get warm for a few minutes. The parents gave us hot chocolate and chatted pleasantly. We never saw their son, and we never told Daddy we had been there.

Even while we were learning in school, we huddled for warmth. We had a one-room school, and in the middle of the room was a pot-bellied stove. The smallest children were seated closest to the stove, where they could keep warm. The rest of us endured varying degrees of cold.

Every day as we walked to school, a big, black car driven by a uniformed chauffeur would pass us. The next county over was Clarke County, where many wealthy people lived. They were descendants of the early settlers, such as the Byrds, Pages, Carters, and Gilpins. We could see a boy in the car, about a year or two older than I. One day, during a driving snowstorm, we were colder than usual because of our thin clothing. The big car appeared, drove past as it always did, but then backed up. The chauffeur opened the door and asked if we would like a ride. Gratefully, we climbed into the car.

"I told the chauffeur to pick you up because it's so cold," the boy said.

We nodded our thanks because our teeth were chattering too much to answer, all the while looking around at the luxurious interior. We had never seen such rich upholstery! The boy introduced himself and asked our names. I cannot remember his first name, but his last name was Gilpin. He said he attended a private school in Winchester. When we told Mama and Daddy that afternoon that we had gotten a ride with the Gilpin boy, they found it hard to believe. However, they knew of the family and we did not, so they thought that we must have been telling the truth.

Luckily, we were picked up a few more times during the school year; we learned an important lesson from this experience. Each time we got into the car, we sensed that the chauffeur was not at all happy about stopping for two ragamuffins. However, since "Master Gilpin" ordered it, he had to obey. For the first time, I became aware of the difference between the rich and poor. I did not resent the young, rich boy, because I knew that he had a kind heart. However, I resented the attitude of the chauffeur. The difference in ours and the Gilpin boy's lifestyles did not seem fair. I could not understand how it happened to be that way. The following year, we did not see the big car again; I suppose the boy must have transferred to another school. He probably never realized how much his lifestyle had impressed me.

THE KIDS NEXT
DOOR

One day, the children who lived on the next farm did not come to school. There were seven in all; some were too young to attend school, but the older ones should have been there. When I got home, I told Mama and asked if they might be sick.

"Their mother died today," Mama said as tears welled up in her eyes.

I was stunned. How could their mama die? She was not even sick. We had just been over to their house the day before. We did not go very often, but when we did, we had fun with the children. We played in the creek and later drank out of the dipper, a coconut shell that hung by the well. Their mother, May, worked in the factory; and their grandmother, Rose Ella, took care of the children. Rose Ella made the best dumplings, and there was nothing we liked better than being asked to stay to supper.

"What made her die?" I asked.

Mama did not answer. Suddenly, she was very busy at the stove. Later, I overheard Mama talking to Rose Ella about a coat hanger and finding May on the bathroom floor in a pool of blood.

Then I heard Rose Ella say, "She just couldn't have another child and keep her job at the factory."

I could not figure out any of it. A year or so later, Mama explained what had happened. May had found out that she was pregnant with her eighth child. She had to work because her husband was "no good" and did not work most of the time. May knew she would have to quit work when her employers learned that she was pregnant, so she tried to abort the baby by inserting a wire coat hanger into her womb. Poor

May; she bled to death on the bathroom floor, leaving seven children without a mother.

My social conscience had been raised at a young age. In particular, I was aware of what was fair and what was not. I have never forgotten that tragedy and the implications it has for a woman's right to choose what happens to her body.

My Teenage Years

My memories of high school are shaky, so I had to contact current school administrators to find my attendance records and report cards. On my first report period in ninth grade, there is a notation: "Dropped Nov. 4, 1935. Nervous breakdown. Reentered Jan. 2, 1936." I was shocked, because I do not recall displaying inappropriate behavior, like squeezing my shoulders, making jerky movements, and grimacing during ninth grade. Despite the two-month absence, I managed to pass ninth grade with a C average.

I do recall my tenth grade year, in 1936 and 1937, when I was fifteen. In fact, I vividly remember my first day walking into a class and exchanging glances with a boy on the other side of the room. It seemed as if an electric current passed between us. This was a new experience for me. Two days later, he handed me a note in the hallway:

> I asked Tommy if he knew your name, and he said it was Virginia Artrip. You probably haven't even noticed me, but I sit next to you in history class. I'm nothing to look at, so you probably haven't even seen me. I have a silly grin and black hair and would make a good scarecrow in someone's garden. Would it be all right with you if I walk to the library with you at study period? If it isn't, please say so. Billy

I said yes and gave him one of my pictures. I had never had a boyfriend. I did not even have a friend, because I was so humiliated about displaying inappropriate physical symptoms in class and then dropping out of school. We exchanged notes every day, and by the end of September, he asked if I would go to the movies with him. I was in love! He was in love!

We shared our love every day in notes, but we also shared our misery. We were probably the two unhappiest students in school, although for different reasons. Billy had come home from school early one day and found his mother in bed with a man when his father was out of town. He had always been very close to his mother, and he had admired and loved her. Now all that was destroyed.

Billy would ride his bicycle to our house after school, and we would sit in the yard or on the porch. We would hold hands and kiss if Daddy was not around. Our relationship deepened on Valentine's Day. Billy was allowed to use the family car to take me to the movies. We found a private spot and parked instead. It had begun to snow, and large flakes were drifting down so slowly it seemed as if they were reluctant to touch the ground. We watched for a while with our arms around each other. Gradually, we began to realize that holding hands and kissing, as we had been doing for six months, was not enough.

We wanted to do more, but Billy did not know how. We were both virgins; however, I knew something about male and female anatomy from reading the big "doctor book" at home. I was able to show him what to do. It was an unforgettable Valentine's night for both of us. There were not many opportunities to make love during the rest of the school year, but we made the most of every chance we got. It never occurred to either of us that I could become pregnant, and we were lucky.

One day, Billy rode to the ice cream shop where I was working part-time after school. When I got off, I rode on his handlebars as we looked for a spot to be alone. At the edge of town, we saw a stately old house far back from the street. It was almost obscured by the huge trees around it. The windows were all shuttered, and it appeared empty.

"Let's go to the porch," Billy said. Holding hands, we climbed the steps and looked around. Dead leaves covered the floor, and spider webs abounded overhead. We sat down on the edge of the porch with our feet on the top step and our arms around each other.

"When we are married, maybe we can buy this place," Billy said. I squeezed his hand in answer, but we both knew we were daydreaming.

We were too young for such all-consuming love. By the following summer, we had broken up. My problems at home and Billy's inability to completely trust me (because of his disillusionment with his mother) were too much for us to overcome. I was totally devastated. His friends told me that he was also. Trying to ease the pain, I wrote poetry—to him, about him, about looking into the future, about when I would forget him.

I'll always believe that our deep love and mutual support kept me from having to drop out of school again, as I had in eighth and ninth grades.

Unfortunately, I do not remember the following year. The only school records I have found are from ninth and tenth grade, then eleventh grade in the fall of 1938, when I was seventeen. What happened to the school year of 1937 and 1938 when I was sixteen? My sisters could never understand why I had no recollection of the things they remembered during that time, even though I was older than they. I am sure I was not "put away" or sent away, for my siblings would have known if I had been missing. I am left with the conclusion that I spent the whole year at home instead of attending school.

When I entered high school the fall of 1938, I was staying with an elderly lady who lived in Winchester near the school, because there was no school bus available. This meant I could walk to the public library every afternoon. I loved browsing through the stacks. Usually, I read four or five books a week.

One night, early in the school year, I was walking home from the library later than usual. It was getting dark when a fire truck passed with sirens blazing. Following the fire truck in his own car was an older boy from school, an eighteen-year-old senior, who lived on the farm next to ours.

He stopped and yelled, "Want to see where the fire is?"

I jumped in his car, and we sped off. The fire turned out to be a minor brush fire, so we started back to town. I noticed a large, fancy flashlight lying on the dashboard. It was a large one, probably powered by five batteries. He said that he had just purchased it. Then he said that he wanted to stop for a minute to see a friend. He pulled up in front of a closed gate. I could see a farmhouse at the end of the lane.

"I'll get out and open the gate," he said.

I watched as he walked toward the gate, noticing his tall and powerful build. Instead of opening the gate, however, he circled in front of the car and came back to the passenger side. He opened the door; and without saying a word, he pushed me back down on the seat, at the same time fumbling with my clothes.

"He's not going to rape me," I remember thinking with the same determination that I felt when I refused to let my father dominate me.

His large size did not intimidate me at all. I pulled up my knees and kicked him as hard as I could in the testicles. He stumbled back, grabbing his crotch and screaming in pain.

As I bolted out the door, I took his flashlight and threw it as far as I could.

"There goes your flashlight!" I yelled as I fled, knowing that he would try to find his new purchase before he would come after me.

That gave me enough time to scurry into the thick bushes that lined the rural road. I could hear him calling to me, then cussing as he tried to find his flashlight. When he gave up on that, he started driving slowly down the road, calling to me. I stayed in the bushes until he gave up and left. Then I walked back to the house where I was staying, feeling triumphant.

I told my parents about the attempted rape when I next talked to them. Daddy said he would talk to the boy's father, but he never did. I was very disappointed and remember thinking that Daddy probably thought I did something to deserve it—another example of his lack of respect for me.

I was still staying with the elderly lady in town, but this lasted only through the second marking period, when the principal and school nurse said that I would have to leave school. They were very caring but also very firm. They finally threatened to expel me if I refused to drop out. I didn't understand why at the time, but I now think it was because my nervous symptoms must have returned in full force.

I could not complete high school. I was again miserable at home because Daddy's mistreatment aggravated my physical condition. I had no job skills, even if my health had permitted me to work. Finally, I could not run away, because there was no place to go.

Despite all these problems, I was fortunate in one major way: my former English teacher, Mr. Browning, pointed out the advantages of not being in a structured classroom environment. Now I could read only what interested me, and I could devote myself to writing poetry. When I read or write poetry, I feel an exquisite emotion. I am moved to joy or sorrow, laughter or tears, because a poet expresses what is in his or her heart, in words that speak to my heart.

That teacher had apparently sensed more about me than I knew about myself. He also loaned me a book written by a friend of his. He told me he valued the book very much and thought I would like it. The book was *Diana Stair*. I immediately identified with the main character, a young woman who fought for the rights of women, organized labor unions, and was not afraid of what others would think of her and her activities.

I had misplaced the book early on, but more than fifty years later, I got a replacement copy through a hard-to-find book service. Reading it from the vantage point of my sixties, I was amazed at Mr. Browning's insight in recognizing a budding Diana Stair in me. Mr. Browning had also read my poetry during high school and made suggestions for improving it. That he took my poetry writing efforts seriously was a terrific morale booster for me.

In spite of this one light in my life when I was seventeen, my life was in limbo.

MAKING A RUN FOR IT

After the attempted rape, I dated other boys my own age to get away from home and to forget Billy. It was late summer, before I entered eleventh grade. One evening, I was invited to a birthday party for a girl I knew, and there I met her older brother, Hendrix. He was tall, handsome, and six years older than I. He asked if he could take me home. After that, he came to see me often. We went for drives, saw movies, or just sat and talked. He was comfortable to be with and made no demands on me. Indeed, his concern was for my happiness.

Shortly after we met, he asked me to marry him. I told him that I wanted to finish school, but we continued to date. When I was forced to quit school, he asked again. I had grown fonder of Hendrix, but I did not love him. However, after a few months of being trapped at home, I agreed to marry him. It was the only way out for me. I assuaged my feelings of guilt by promising myself that I would learn to love him and be a good wife.

A Church of the Brethren minister married us on January 18, 1939. The ceremony took place in the minister's study. Daddy did not attend. Mama and I both cried—she because she was happy for me, I because I was so unsure of the future.

I seemed happy to all our friends and family, as well as to Hendrix. I was determined that no one would ever know that I did not love Hendrix. We lived on Chapel Hill farm, near Boyce, Virginia, where Hendrix was a herdsman who helped to raise purebred Angus cattle. Hendrix would take the Black Angus to cattle shows, frequently winning blue ribbons.

While Hendrix was busy at work, I was busy learning to be a housewife. I borrowed books from the library and learned the proper way to set a table. I bought cookbooks and learned how to cook. After painting and decorating the rooms in our house, I planted flowers and made a rock garden. I also enjoyed time to myself, for I had ample opportunity to write poetry and read as many books as I wanted. Hendrix was sympathetic about my desire to continue my studies at home. His love and tenderness were providing the healing I needed.

Then I learned that I was pregnant. We had been married a little over a year, and I was not ready to be a mother. I was panic stricken, but Hendrix was thrilled. I pretended to be happy about the pregnancy. Unfortunately, I had more than morning sickness to contend with. My blood pressure shot up to a dangerous level. My legs and the rest of my body began to swell. My doctor explained that I might not be able to carry the baby full term. On January 21, 1941, Kathleen Ellen was born two months premature and died soon thereafter. Hendrix was devastated. I felt a sense of relief along with a terrible sense of loss. My doctor talked to me about having my tubes tied because the risks of another pregnancy were so high. I wanted to try again for Hendrix's sake.

The next time I was pregnant, Dr. Allen had to induce labor at six months because of health complications, and the child, another girl, was stillborn. There were two more pregnancies. The fourth I managed to carry eight months. The child, whom I named Rebecca, lived only five days. When I awoke the morning after giving birth, I could not see the nurse or the breakfast tray. I was blind!

By the time I left the hospital two weeks later, I was relieved that I could distinguish between light and dark. Within three months, my normal sight had returned, and I quickly had my tubes tied. No more would I tempt Fate. Hendrix was heartbroken, but he was very understanding.

Blind

"Wake up," I told myself.
"Just try once more.
You are awake now,
can't you see the light?
It must be day,
for all the sounds around
are different from
the silences of night."

"So you're awake now. Good.
then here's your tray."
Somewhere in the blackness,
soft and kind.
It was my nurse, *the one
who came by day*.
And then I realized
that I was blind.

REFLECTIONS ON MY FATHER

During the early years of my marriage, I had ample time for introspection, time to sort out the past. Most important to understand was my hatred for my father. Why had he treated me as he had? Why would he tell me over and over, "I'm going to conquer you, if it's the last thing I do"? He already controlled Mama.

Often, when he was punishing me, he would shout, "You're just like your grandmother!"

Daddy's mother, Grandmother Alice, left her husband because he was having an affair with a fifteen-year-old girl, whom he later married. My grandmother had inherited some money from her father, but she had to leave it all behind. She also had to leave behind her three young children. Around the turn of the century, there was no way that a woman leaving her husband would be granted custody of their children. According to Daddy and his siblings, their mother had abandoned them.

Grandmother Alice had gone to New Mexico, where she homesteaded. At first she lived in a grass hut, built partly underground. Gradually, she prospered, accumulated cattle, and then traded a herd of cows for a ranch in Oklahoma. Daddy had visited her in New Mexico when he was seventeen. He hopped freight trains and worked his way west. During my childhood, he often talked about the Indians he met on the way, but he did not talk about the reunion with his mother. I got the impression that there were no happy memories connected with the visit.

When I was young, Daddy's constant reminder that I was just like my grandmother puzzled me. I knew she had abandoned her children, but then she would send us gifts, and Mama would read us her letters; I was torn about what to believe. I recall that she sent us a beautiful beaded basket made by the Indians that we played with until it was destroyed. When I was very little, she also sent a string of pink coral beads that just fit around my neck. Somehow they managed to survive, and I gave them to my grandniece, Nicole Campbell, when she was born.

I also had a couple of faded snapshots showing her standing erect, with her head held high. She did come to visit when I was a child, and I have vivid memories of staying at her rented apartment. Grandma had a firm, no-nonsense attitude, did not smile often, and did not make unnecessary conversation, but I knew she loved me and loved being with me.

When I learned Grandma's history after I was grown, I realized that I was very much like her, and not just because my middle name is Alice. She was intelligent and independent; she made her own decisions and was her own person. In fact, when she realized her second marriage was a mistake, she did not divorce her husband. Instead, she built a second house on the other side of her Oklahoma ranch and moved him over there. They lived in separate houses until she died in 1934, when she was sixty-eight.

Had Daddy tried to conquer her by conquering me? After many years of thinking about this question, I have concluded that the answer is yes. Daddy transferred his hatred of his mother to me because I reminded him of her. Her focus and courage had found their way into the deepest core of my being, and I could not be conquered either.

Daddy was not all bad, however. During my days of introspection, I also remembered his positive traits. He taught me about kindness to neighbors and fairness in business dealings. I remember when a neighbor's barn burned down. Daddy gave him a check, even though we also needed the money. He helped neighbors in other ways when they were in need, always quietly and unobtrusively.

One day, a man came to buy a horse from him. He liked one particular horse, but Daddy told him that something was wrong with it. I do not recall what the problem was, but it was not obvious. After the prospective buyer left without purchasing it, a friend of Daddy's who was also there admonished him. "Let the buyer beware," the friend said. "You didn't need to tell him there was anything wrong with the horse."

Daddy thanked him for his advice.

Sometime later, that same friend came to look for a horse and picked out one he liked. Daddy delivered it to his farm. The next day, the man came to see Daddy, and he was very upset.

"Frank, why didn't you tell me that horse couldn't get up when he lay down?"

With a straight face, Daddy replied, "Well, you told me about letting the buyer beware."

Then he took his truck and picked up the horse and exchanged it for another that was healthy. It was a lesson I never forgot.

As my father grew older, his need for power appeared to decrease, at least as far as I could tell. The first hint I had that Daddy was mellowing toward me was when I was thirty-one and working in Orlando. He bought me a used car. It was an unexpected blessing.

Later, when he was in his seventies and we were walking in the garden with Mama, he put his arm around my waist. I was surprised, because Daddy did not display affection.

"I'm sorry I mistreated you," he said. That was all.

Gradually, I began to understand and forgive my father, because he was a tormented man. But I could never come to love him—or forget.

FINDING MYSELF

After I regained my sight, I completely reassessed my life. I was not yet twenty-five years old. I realized now that I needed to find fulfillment other than raising children in the years ahead. Hendrix was a loving husband; he worked hard and did not expect me to work outside the house. However, I knew that I could not be a "taker" for the rest of my life. Somehow, I had to find a way to contribute my share. I had no marketable skills, so I bought a secondhand typewriter and a typing manual. Then I typed everything from the grocery lists to articles in the newspaper, just to practice.

Soon, I began to do some work for Hendrix's boss, R. J. Funkhouser, who raised expensive registered Hereford cattle. R. J., as everyone called him, was a self-made millionaire who had bought and restored five homes that had been owned by the family of George Washington. He lived in one of them—the former home of Samuel Washington, brother of the president—which he had furnished with purchases from the William Randolph Hearst estate.

R. J. helped me out of my self-conscious shell by insisting that I could do things I had never done before. I started slowly, as secretary in a one-person office for his artificial breeding laboratory. I would not have to worry about interacting with the public or other employees, except for the veterinarian. I believed I could handle the work. This was a perfect job for someone with low self-esteem, and when the lab burned down a year later, it marked an important change in my life.

After the fire, R. J. began assigning me various jobs, none of which I had ever done before. The first one was to do a survey for his newspaper, the *Jefferson Republican*.

"I can't do that," I protested. "It means going up to perfect strangers and asking them questions!"

"You can do it," R. J. said confidently, putting his arm around my shoulder. He would not take no for an answer. His faith in me gave me the push I needed; I decided that if someone as successful as R. J. chose me for the job, maybe I could do it. I would pretend that I knew what I was doing, and that would calm my nerves. It worked, and R. J. was happy with the survey results.

After that, for the next three years I was more or less on call for whatever he needed me to do. I would take groups of people on tours of his historic home; I filled in when a clerk in his upscale shop became ill; I sold advertising for the newspaper when a salesman took time off; and most importantly for me, I wrote stories for the newspaper. Each time I tackled an unfamiliar task, I gained more confidence, until I decided that I could do anything anyone else could do, unless it took specialized training. I could begin anew, because a great man believed in me. Now, after twelve years of marriage, I believed in myself. I was ready to make the next very difficult decision in my life.

Goodbyes

Goodbyes are always sudden,
As everybody knows.
We never really hear them
Until the whistle blows.

SMELLING THE APPLE BLOSSOMS

I wanted more than ever to be a good wife to Hendrix; but for the years we were together, I suffered from migraine headaches. They were coming more frequently and with greater intensity. Doctors ruled out any physiological basis. After much soul-searching, I decided that my headaches were caused by the lie I was living. I was pretending to love Hendrix as a husband, when I loved him more as a brother or a best friend. I shared my insight with my doctor. He told me, "You should leave Hendrix, or I will not be responsible. The mind can blank out in self-defense, and you could end up with amnesia."

"You get amnesia from getting hit on the head," I argued.

"You can also get amnesia from too much stress," he countered.

I did not believe the amnesia theory, and I didn't want to make Hendrix suffer for something that was my fault. Then the incidents of amnesia began. I got into the car to go to the post office one day, about a fifteen-minute drive. The next thing I knew, I was at the counter, and the clerk was addressing me. I looked at the people in line, some of whom I knew. No one was looking at me strangely, so I figured I must have behaved normally as I waited in line. But the time since I left home was a total blank.

There was one other similar episode, and I was convinced that the doctor was right. Also, what about the times I blanked out during high school? For months, I hardly slept. At one point I considered suicide. I was totally overwhelmed by my dread of hurting Hendrix.

It was a heart-wrenching decision to make. Hendrix had been a good husband and friend. He had supported me in whatever I wanted, and he loved me very much. I would hurt him terribly if I left.

A short time later, I was walking along the lane from our house to the mailbox when I suddenly smelled apple blossoms. It was midwinter. I stopped walking and breathed deeply of the sweet perfume. There was no mistaking the smell of apple blossoms, although nothing was blooming that time of year. As I stood there wondering, a feeling of complete peace came over me.

Suddenly, I knew that everything would be all right. I no longer felt torn. I knew what had to be done, and I did it as quickly and painlessly as possible. In addition to addressing Christmas cards and buying gifts, I wrote letters of explanation to close friends and family. I was going to Florida on my doctor's orders because of the headaches.

I did not tell Hendrix. No one except a close friend and my sister Juanita knew about my plans. I left a letter for Hendrix, explaining as best I could why I believed that I needed to end our marriage. I mailed the other letters on my way to the train station. I bought a one-way ticket to Kissimmee, Florida, and took one hundred dollars from our checking account. It was January of 1951. I was thirty years old. I planned to stay with friends until I could find a job.

Within two weeks, Hendrix was there to bring me home. He was adamant about not going back unless I went with him. He would lose his job if he stayed away too long, and yet he would not budge. I went back, making it clear to him that I was doing this only so he would not lose his job. He wanted me back so badly that he did not care why I came.

Leaving Hendrix the first time—having to tell him that I never loved him as a wife should and that I had been lying all those years—had been traumatizing for me. Now I would have to do it all over again. This time I had to make sure he did not know where I was going, so I didn't tell anyone in my family. I did tell one close friend where I could be reached in case of a family emergency. This time I went to Orlando. I rented a room about a block away from beautiful Eola Park, in the center of town. Every chance I got, I would walk down to the lake, sit on a bench, and enjoy the solitude. I was starting a new life, and I wanted to make sure I headed in the right direction.

I loved writing for The *Jefferson Republican*, the paper owned by R. J. Funkhouser, so I applied for a job on the Orlando *Sentinel-Star*. The newspaper was based in a big, old, wood-framed building with paddle fans overhead and no air-conditioning. At that time, only three buildings in Orlando had air-conditioning—two big downtown department stores and the Catholic church.

I was hired to revive a shopping column the publisher's wife had written before she died. I wrote in a light, chatty style and added a four-line verse at the top of the column, such as:

> Live-in Baby-Sitter
> If you would like to leave the house
> To do some shopping, maybe,
> Just catch your unsuspecting spouse
> And let him mind the baby!

"Shopping with Jeanne" grew to a full three columns within a few months.

I rented a small studio apartment near the office and set about adjusting to my new life. It was such a relief to be rid of the headaches. The month before I left Hendrix for the first time, I had ten headaches and lost two or three pounds with each from vomiting and cold sweats. Now, for the first time in years, I was free of the debilitating attacks.

Then one day, I opened the door to find Hendrix. The husband of my friend felt sorry for him and had given him my address! He stayed two weeks before I could convince him that I was not coming back.

"How can you want me back when you know I don't love you?" I asked.

"It was always so interesting," he replied, half laughing and half crying.

We had an amicable divorce, and I refused to take any money or things except for my personal items, my books, and my typewriter. Hendrix did remarry after some time, and he and his second wife had a son and three daughters. I am so grateful that he found happiness, because hurting Hendrix was one of the most painful episodes of my life.

Patience

And this is all
I know, alas.
Though tears may fall,
They, too, will pass

FALLING IN LOVE

In 1952, after a year of working for the Orlando *Sentinel-Star*, I decided I wanted to study journalism at Columbia University. I had been offered a job in New York, which I accepted. At the same time, my sister Juanita, who had opened a restaurant in Winchester, Virginia, after she got divorced, found that she was pregnant. She asked if I would postpone my move to New York to help her with the restaurant until she had the baby. Her baby was born in October of 1952; by March of 1953, I was ready to move. One week before I was to leave, a man named Ross walked into the restaurant to inquire about an accident nearby. He decided to eat lunch, and I waited on him. He also stayed for dinner; the rest is history.

I was very attracted to Ross because of his engaging smile and soul-searching eyes. He was very handsome. I felt the chemistry between us right away. What kept me attracted to him was his tenderness and depth of character. During long hours of conversation, I learned that he was separated from his wife and had two little girls whom he loved very much. He also owned an insurance agency that he did not love very much. Just before I met him, he had bought a truck and was delivering new cars until he could decide what he was going to do with his life. He said he never planned to marry again.

I moved to New York the next week, and Ross followed me there. I was very surprised and happy to see him. We went to dinner and talked for hours. Again, he commented that he never planned to marry again. I patted his hand and reassured him, "You're safe with me." But I thought, "He's protesting too much!"

Ross asked if he could take me out to breakfast the next morning, Easter morning, April 5. On the elevator ride downstairs in the morning, he proposed, and I accepted ... when I finally stopped laughing! I just knew that Ross was the love of my life.

I found us an apartment near Columbia University, and Ross continued to deliver new cars up and down the east coast as we planned our new life together. We had not married yet because Ross's divorce was not final. Our best-laid plans for living in New York went astray. Within a short time, I had to go back to Winchester, Virginia, where I grew up and knew the doctors, for a hysterectomy. Because of my health problems, I had to temporarily set aside my dream of studying. I was used to disappointments, and I knew that this was not a permanent setback.

After recovering from surgery, I decided that a move to Florida would be better for my recovery than a move to New York. I convinced Ross that we should live in Orlando and hoped that he would love Florida as much as I did. It worked!

Ross had been schooled in architecture and engineering. When we moved to Orlando in November of 1953, he took brush-up lessons in drafting. Within a short time, he had a job with the city of Orlando as a drainage design engineer.

A Place I Belong

Shortly after we were married, Ross and I became members of the Unitarian Church in Orlando. This came about quite by accident; it began when the church offered a program on archeology one Wednesday evening. We attended because I have always been fascinated by the subject. In fact, my earliest memory—I was only three years old—is of King Tut's tomb. I remember the Winchester *Evening Star*'s two-page spread of sepia-colored photos of the beautiful furnishings found in the tomb.

My first archeological dig occurred when I was about eight years old. My sister Juanita and I decided to explore the old graveyard at the far end of our property. It belonged to another family and had been there when we bought the farm. Mama had cleaned up most of the trash and straightened up the tombstones.

"We might find some treasure in the graves," I told Juanita.

We got the posthole digger and waited until Mama was in the back of the house doing laundry. Then we hid behind the largest tombstone and started to dig. The posthole digger was too heavy for either of us to lift, so we each held on to one side and managed to dig a hole about six inches deep. Suddenly, our digger struck something.

We've hit a body!" I whispered in panic, and we took off running.

Mama realized that we had been quiet for too long and came to check on us. She found us trembling under the porch. We quickly confessed, and Mama ran off to check the grave. We found her laughing as she held up an old shoe that had been covered with the trash many years earlier, but that we had thought was a body!

I was thinking about my first dig as I browsed through the various brochures and articles at the table in the foyer before the meeting. I had never heard of the Unitarian Church before and was curious. I saw no references to sin, redemption, Holy Ghost, or the rest of it. Instead, the articles I read stressed justice, compassion, brotherhood, and service to others. There was no requirement of believing in Jesus. This was a church? Incredible! I told Ross that we should attend a Sunday morning service, which we did on Mother's Day.

As a child, I was used to listening to our hypocritical minister preach very long and emotional sermons on Mother's Day. He and his wife had about a dozen children. She always sat at the back of the church, looking tired and wan, wearing the same old coat year after year. I knew one of their daughters, and one Sunday she had invited me to go home with her after church. The "man of God" sat in an easy chair and ordered his wife to get him some coffee. He took a sip and then spat it all over the floor. Then he yelled that it was too hot and ordered her to clean it up. Obediently, she did as she was told. I never went back to that house again.

The morning Ross and I went to the Unitarian Church on Mother's Day, the Reverend John Fuller began his sermon by pointing out that mothers are concerned about the mental health of their families. The rest of the sermon focused on the mentally ill patients held in the county jail because there was no mental hospital in Orlando. Many in the audience were shocked to learn this and were inspired to take action. Ross and I immediately joined the effort to get a hospital, and, more importantly, we joined the church. That the first minister of the church had been a woman probably also influenced me to become a member!

Beauty and Truth

I lived for Beauty
And not for Truth,
But that was in
My foolish youth.

As I grew older
And knew my duty,
I lived for Truth
And not for Beauty.

Now that my life
Is almost done,
I know that Beauty
And Truth are one.

JUSTICE FOR TOMMY

In Orlando I learned more lessons about life's unfairness. At that time, the "old-timers" ran the Orange County Road and Bridge Department, under Superintendent Whitney W. Wolf. He and almost all of his employees maintained control because they were members of the Ku Klux Klan and everyone feared them. For years there were whispered reports of stealing and payoffs.

I did not know enough to be afraid when I was employed as secretary to the newly hired county engineer, Fred W. DeWitt, in June of 1958. The county commissioners had hired DeWitt over the protests of Wolf because the county had substandard streets that had never been approved by county inspectors. As a result, many streets were not the required width and did not have proper drainage, among other problems. Wolf was not fired, however—and that should have been my first clue that Wolf was considered untouchable. I thought he looked and acted like a typical "redneck": crude, swaggering, and bigoted. I remember telling my husband, Ross, that DeWitt was going to need all the help he could get if he was going to straighten out that office.

It started on Monday, July 14, 1958, when E. C. Yarborough, supervisor of the survey crews, said that one of his crew chiefs, Tommy Wilkerson, was out ill. The survey crews worked out of our office; I kept their personnel and payroll records, so I automatically became involved in the situation. The next day, Yarborough reported that Tommy was still out ill. Other crew members remarked that they were surprised, because Tommy never took sick leave, but they added that he was also so honest that they did not doubt his word. On Wednesday, Yarborough said he would go to Tommy's house to get him to see a doctor. He found a terrified Tommy, perspiring and shaking.

Later, Yarborough told us that Tommy kept saying, "They are going to get me; don't let them get me, Mr. Yarborough."

"When I asked who 'they' were," Yarborough continued, "Tommy did mention Jim Drury, Wolf's shop foreman."

Instead of going to see a doctor, as Yarborough had hoped, Tommy went to his sister's house in Pine Hills, outside Orlando. His sister and her family were away on vacation at the time. When Yarborough went to check on Tommy Thursday morning, he found the sister's house unlocked, and there was no sign of Tommy or his car. Yarborough said he was concerned and called Tommy's brother, who lived in Jacksonville. The brother left for Orlando immediately.

At the same time, Drury came back from lunch and announced to the group in the office that Tommy had called him at home during lunch and threatened him. "He said, 'I'm going to get you,' and hung up."

All of us in the office were shocked and protested that this certainly did not sound like Tommy, who was quiet and mild mannered. I noticed that Yarborough did not join our protestations.

Drury continued. "Tommy didn't give his name, but I know Tommy's voice. If Tommy is acting so strangely, anything is possible."

I was suspicious.

When Tommy's brother arrived shortly thereafter, he wanted to call in a missing person report to the Orange County Sheriff's Department. Drury stopped him, saying that Wolf wanted to talk to them first. That call was delayed for three hours. Another thing struck me as odd: from the time Tommy's brother arrived at our office, I never noticed him speaking with Yarborough—yet Yarborough had been the one who called him in the first place.

Everyone was upset about Tommy's disappearance, especially when we learned from his brother that Tommy had left his watch, billfold, and dog tags, among other things, on the coffee table at his sister's house. We also learned that Tommy had handed his paycheck to his sister's neighbor Wednesday afternoon and asked the neighbor to give it to her when she returned from her vacation. I feared foul play and called Deputy Sam Bush of the Orange County Sheriff's Department when I got home from work.

Tommy's body was discovered Friday afternoon. I read about it Saturday morning in the Orlando *Sentinel*, August 19, 1958.

Two mysteries jelled into one solution yesterday when the body of an Orlando man found on the edge of a canal was linked with a car abandoned two days ago after it crashed into a nearby fence.

The body, tentatively identified as that of Thomas J. Wilkerson, 911 Sunniland Drive, about 28, was found on the bank of a canal near Highway 17 within the Brunswick Georgia city limits.

Wilkerson had worked for the Orange County Road and Bridge Department for the past three years. He had left Orlando on Monday to go on vacation, Whitney W. Wolf, superintendent of the department, said last night.

Police found no identification on the body, only two packages of cigarettes and a car key.

The old model car was found two nights ago after it crashed into a fence dividing the highway lanes. No driver could he found.

Officers took the key from the dead man's pocket and placed it in the ignition of the unclaimed car. They matched. Papers found inside the car led to the conclusion that the body was that of Wilkerson, Police Capt. Bob Lyns said. Police speculate that the man suffered an attack, causing him to crash through the fence, then wander to the canal in the dark and fall in.

An unofficial autopsy report revealed that death occurred from drowning with no evidence of foul play. A brother is traveling to Brunswick from Florida to identify the body.

Wolf said that Tommy left Orlando two days ago en route to Illinois.

I could not believe what I was reading! Wolf, who was not even Tommy's boss (Tommy and I worked for DeWitt), had told the reporter that Tommy had left to go on vacation, but this was not true; I would have known if Tommy had decided to go on vacation, because I took care of the payroll. Besides, Yarborough reported that Tommy was sick, and I had marked him as being on sick leave when he did not come to work.

To make matters even more bizarre, Tommy's brother told me that he had never talked to anyone at the newspaper, and he certainly would not have said that Tommy was going to Illinois, because he had no idea where Tommy had gone. Also, when I spoke to Yarborough, he was very vague about the details. Now I was certain that Tommy had met with foul play, but I did not know why.

Although the case was soon closed, I continued my investigation. I knew that I had to be careful, however, because before Tommy's murder, one of the engineers had told me that our office was used for Ku Klux Klan meetings at night and that he had found KKK literature around in the mornings. Someone else had told me that most of the men in Wolf's department were KKK members. Therefore, I decided to stay in constant contact with Deputy Sam Bush and FBI agent Charles Robichaud during my investigation, figuring that this was the best life insurance I could get. Little did I know that Bush would be of no help.

My queries began to pay off when I found a girlfriend of one of the men who worked in the Road and Bridge Department. Word was that she was a cashier in a Winn-Dixie store, and I started making it my business to shop and then check out through her lane. After a while, I mentioned where I worked, and we would chat each time I was at the store. One day, she let something slip about the way things were going in the R and B Department. As a result of our developing friendship, I learned about the corruption of Wolf and his men. She told me in private conversations after work that many men in the department bought all kinds of items for themselves and charged them to the county. For example, they purchased radiators, seat covers, and tires for their cars; tile, light fixtures, and paint for their apartments. They also took items already in stock for their own use at home.

The girlfriend's information was verified when a former secretary at the county office told me about fake receipts for the missing stock.

When the secretary had told Wolf about hundreds of dollars worth of missing tires, she said that Wolf had brought her receipts for these tires and told her to put any dates on them as long as they were not Sundays. Soon afterward, she was fired for "incompetence." Suspecting corruption, she hid the receipts on her last day.

Now, as secretary myself, I had access to everything in the office. With the former secretary's directions, I found the receipts at the back of a file cabinet drawer. I copied the information but left the receipts where they were. Then I began to theorize about why Tommy Wilkerson had been killed: perhaps he had found out about all of the stealing and refused to go along with it.

In the meantime, I noticed that other people in the office were becoming unfriendly to me, perhaps because they were afraid to talk to me. That I was continuing my investigation into Tommy's death was no secret. I did not share what I had been learning, but there were plenty of people watching and listening when I made phone calls for appointments or information.

More importantly, I made no secret of my disgust when the White Citizens Council of Alabama came to Orange County and began stirring up racial hatred with statements like, "If segregation is good enough for cows and hogs, why ain't it good enough for humans?" My protest letter to the editor was published in the Orlando *Sentinel*, near the end of September. People in the office spoke of me as a "nigger-lover," and now they became very rude to me. The atmosphere at the office was ugly.

Then, after holding the job for only five months, I was fired. The county commissioners of Orange County forced DeWitt to fire me on November 17 because "county employees should not become involved in controversial issues."

Shortly thereafter, I decided to go to Deputy Bush with all of the information I had concerning Tommy Wilkerson's murder. I was frustrated and puzzled when nothing came of my efforts, until I learned that Sheriff Dave Starr, Bush's boss, was notorious for his racist attitude and his powerful role in the KKK. There was no official I could trust.

A month later, my husband and I found out that the KKK had not forgotten about me. About 7:30 a.m., Ross was driving the little Austin Minor car that I usually drove. An Orange County dump truck followed Ross for a few miles, then passed him and cut him off. Ross had to slam on the brakes to avoid an accident, so he could not get a tag number as the truck sped away. We reported this incident to the police, but we were not surprised when nothing came of our report. I knew that Ross and I had to take precautions, but I refused to be intimidated by these thugs. Now that I look back, I do not know if I was being foolhardy or just focused!

On another occasion, an unknown person threw broken glass and eggs at our house. At no time in the following years did any official look into Tommy's death, no matter what I did to raise the issue with officials. I was profoundly disappointed and frustrated. This had been an important but bitter lesson.

I understand now, forty-eight years later, that the Orlando police department has a Cold Case Unit. I hope that giving my notes now to the department will ensure justice for Tommy Wilkerson.

The Sun

The day is spent, the setting sun,
  With long and rosy fingers,
Lays its caress on everyone
  As lovingly it lingers.
Though loath to leave the world alone,
  Without its loving care,
The light slips quite away from sight
  Before we are aware.
But then the dawn creeps slowly in;
  The black turns soon to gray.
And now the world will smile again.
  It is a lovely day.

FIGHTING CITY HALL

In the summer of 1959, I planned Sunday programs at the Unitarian Church we attended while the minister was on vacation. One Sunday, I asked Tony Chastain, a gadfly-type radio talk show host, to speak about a social issue that might motivate our members to become more active in the community. He told us about the pending Port Authority bill for Orange County, which would give almost unlimited power to the "old courthouse gang." We learned that if the bill were passed, the members, officers, and employees of the Port Authority could also make franchise agreements with the Authority to have their own businesses—such as car rentals, taxi and limousine service, even restaurant operation—provide services without other bids being required. Neither their meetings nor the minutes of their meetings had to be made public. The Authority was not even required to make its audits public!

Chastain urged us to make voters aware of the dangers of the bill. Six of us decided to take up the challenge. The next day, we tried to get a copy of the bill and found out it was being kept a secret. Finally, we managed to get a copy without the knowledge of the bill's supporters. Ross went to the Port Authority office. The clerk knew that Ross worked for the city, so she assumed that he was on official business and gave him a copy. I cut stencils of the thirty-eight legal-sized pages, and we made copies on the church mimeograph machine.

I suggested that our small group of six should be named the Citizens' Committee for Good Government (CCGG), and we adopted the name. First, we studied other port authorities, noting their strengths and weaknesses; then we put together a flier. We also made it our business to attend public meetings whenever our county commissioners or state legislators were speaking so we could ask pointed questions about the bill's dangers. In the meantime, we made numerous telephone calls to voters.

As the date of the referendum approached, supporters of the bill bought a full-page ad in the Orlando *Sentinel*. The message read that if voters did not support the bill, Orlando would be in the backwash of civilization. The entire page was filled with names of the supporters: the rich and powerful in Orange County, including the *Sentinel* publisher. We quickly raised enough money for a quarter-page ad, in which we reprinted our flier.

On the night of the election, our small group gathered at one of our houses and nervously awaited the results. It was madness to think that we could defeat a bill supported by so many powerful people. Still, we were hopeful. When the votes were tallied, we learned that the bill had been defeated by a two-to-one margin. We had done it! This was a true David and Goliath story. We had killed the monster.

After beating the Port Authority bill, we decided to tackle another important issue in Orlando politics. We began to research whether Orlando needed a new airport. To begin, we were shocked to learn that the brother-in-law of one of the county commissioners owned the tract of land that the Commission planned to purchase for the new airport—at a cost of twelve million dollars, a vast amount of money at the time.

In the course of our research, we also learned that the base of the Strategic Air Command (SAC) was on land owned by the city of Orlando and that this land could also be used for commercial flights. Armed with this information, we approached the Orlando City Council and suggested they ask the Air Force for permission to use the SAC base for commercial flights. The request was made to the Secretary of the Air Force in Washington, DC, and permission was granted.

A short time later, Ross and I attended a dinner for Governor Leroy Collins in Orlando. Among those at our table were a local judge and a vice-president of a local bank. The talk turned to the defeat of the Port Authority bill.

"Is it true," I asked, "that the Citizens for Good Government defeated that bill?"

"You'd better believe it," the banker replied. "When that name comes up in conversation ..." He did not complete the sentence. Instead, he drew his finger across his throat and made a gurgling sound to indicate a throat being cut. It was obvious he did not know I was a member of the CCGG, and I decided not to enlighten him. Indeed, I was proud of my accomplishments as a member of a small group who fought city hall and won!

THE POWER OF ONE

O ur church in Boca Raton had started a Unitarian Fellowship in the community during the 1960s, and many of the members were active in the community on an individual basis. Because of this, a delegation from Pearl City, the city's black section, came to our newly formed social action committee in 1965 with a request for help.

The academically disadvantaged black students were having difficulty keeping up with the white students in the newly desegregated Boca Raton High School. As a result, the black students were threatening to drop out. Wayne Rogers and I, members of the Social Action Committee, and students at FAU recruited volunteers from the college to tutor these black students full time during Christmas vacation. This crash program was credited with preventing any of the students from dropping out of school that year.

Also that year, we established a tutorial center for students who needed supervised help with homework. The help came from volunteers at area schools and colleges. Most of the students in this program were blacks from Pearl City and Latinos who lived in the Garden Apartments section of town.

Through the tutorial program, volunteers learned that there were many other social problems not being addressed. At my urging, the Unitarian Board of Directors voted to open the South County Neighborhood Center at Boca Raton on March 4, 1968. I was the volunteer coordinator and director for the first three years of the Center. SCNC was soon established as a community, non-profit organization, operated entirely by volunteers—seventy-six the first year! It was a massive undertaking and my proudest achievement. I was also a full-time reporter in Fort Lauderdale at the time. I do not know how I managed to do it all.

I taught and supervised the volunteers. In fact, three volunteers had been assigned to SCNC from Volunteers to America (VTA), at my request. One of the most important programs we started was a day care center for young children of mothers who had to work, most of them as maids for wealthy white women. This became the Florence Fuller Day Care Center.

The SCNC volunteers performed many specific duties, some that one would expect at our center, such as transportation, but also some that one would not expect. For instance, one afternoon, two young volunteers grabbed a can of Raid to kill a swarm of bees that were found in the walls of a client's house! Our volunteers were so compassionate that they even brought heaters from their own homes to help families during a cold spell. Even more remarkable, wives of two professors from FAU washed clothes for a client because she had a broken arm and could not care for her home and four children.

Our first year was a great success. One of the VTA workers—Shoji Oue, of Japan—decided to stay a second year and became a full-time resident volunteer and coordinator of youth services. When Shoji discovered a group of black teenage musicians under a banyan tree in Pearl City, he named the group "The Soul Seekers Band." The teenagers were writing and playing music with an old guitar, an automobile fender, and a garbage can! With the help of SCNC, the group acquired a set of drums and an electric guitar. Under Shoji's supervision, they practiced daily for several weeks. Soon, they found that they could earn twenty dollars a night playing at local parties. Shortly before school ended for the summer, The Soul Seekers Band won first place in a talent show at Boca Raton Junior High School.

Shoji also organized monthly picnics at Spanish River Park. An average of 140 children from Pearl City and the Garden Apartments, ages seven to fourteen, attended these outings at the park. Many of these children had never even seen the ocean. They integrated the Boca Raton Beach, despite the concerns of the director of Parks and Recreation that the white people of Boca were not used to seeing blacks on their beach.

"Can't you just have half of them one month and half the next month?" the director, James Rutherford, asked me plaintively. I refused the suggestion.

Indeed, although many people worked for and supported SCNC those early years, some city officials resented the program.

"There's no poverty in Boca Raton," one official told me, "and besides, you're calling attention to it by having that center right across from City Hall."

Nevertheless, we persevered. Volunteers taught classes in sewing and electronics. I taught a class entitled "What to Do If the Police Stop You." One of the students credited my class with saving his life. The situation occurred when a small group of black children had gone into a neighborhood bowling alley next to Pearl City to play pinball. They had put their quarters in the machines and were ready to begin playing when the manager ordered them to leave. They agreed to go but first wanted their quarters back. Instead of returning their money, the manager called the police. The officer who responded pulled out his gun, and the children began filing out. Not satisfied with their pace, he began pushing them, and one of the oldest boys, who felt responsible for the younger children, fell to the ground.

"Mrs. Snyder, you saved my life," he told me the next day. "The officer was calling us 'mother fuckers' and 'coons' and other dirty names. I was so mad that when my hands felt a rock where I fell, my first thought was to hit him with it. He had his gun in my back, and I know he would have shot me if I had picked up that rock."

Other needs of the children were met in 1970 by Project You, a "Listening to Children" program staffed by trained volunteers. Most importantly, the staff learned to be non-judgmental as they listened. In this way, counseling and other services were provided for pre-delinquent children who had been referred by schools and ministers.

Ten years passed, and most of the assistance that SCNC had offered was now offered by other agencies in Boca Raton and Delray Beach. This was not true of assistance needed for the elderly; therefore, the Center shifted its focus to that segment of the population. Thanks to the extraordinary generosity of Benjamin and Mae Volen in funding SCNC's current building, the center was renamed the Mae Volen Center. More than 4,500 seniors a year receive services, ranging from in-home care to transportation. I see the little white and blue buses everywhere seniors need to be—in shopping centers, in the parking lots of clinics. They provide 80,000 rides a year. Each bus is a reminder that I was privileged to start and head the South County Neighborhood Center at Boca Raton until it was on its own feet.

I was especially honored when Governor Lawton Chiles designated me as the recipient of the "Florida's Finest" award in 1996 to "Thank you and commend you for your dedication to your community and its members, but especially for your hard work with the South County Neighborhood Center." I am one lucky lady!

Riches

Count not your wealth in silver
Nor reckon it in gold,
Or else you may discover,
When you are bent and old,
Riches are not made of things
That can be bought and sold.

SHOJI

Ross and I met Shoji Oue in August of 1968, when he arrived from Japan as one of the first Volunteers to America (VTAs) to work at the South County Neighborhood Center. These carefully screened young people—Shoji was twenty-one—came to work with poor people in ghettoes and migrant camps. We had three volunteers that year, and as their supervisor, I came to know and appreciate the conditions they endured. In addition to the difficulties they had trying to help the people solve their problems, they lived and worked with rats, palmetto bugs, and roaches!

Therefore, Ross and I soon gave each volunteer a key to our house for R and R, just to get a little rest, take a nap, and "recharge their psychic batteries." Our VTA workers cherished their time there. Thus, we came to know and love them, especially Shoji, who stayed a second year to work at the Center with us.

I have detailed some of the work Shoji did with the poor in Boca Raton with the South County Neighborhood Center. It is time to explain further why we continued to be astonished by his boundless energy and enthusiasm for project after project. For example, in 1969, when SCNC received a grant for a juvenile delinquency prevention program, he worked with director Doris Abraham. In addition to founding The Soul Seekers Band, as explained in the earlier chapter, Shoji also organized a basketball team that was unbeaten in the area. He taught dozens of children to swim. In the summer, he took children to swim at what is now Lynn University and to Florida Atlantic University, when he learned that black children were excluded from the city's program. Then there were the little-league-type baseball, volleyball, and ping-pong teams he started and supervised.

On August 29, 1970, Shoji planned a picnic for the children as his going-away party. The Boca Raton Jaycees helped with the party and announced that they had chosen Shoji as "'Outstanding Young Man of the Year." They gave him a plaque, which read: "His dedication to service to all humanity will serve as a lasting reminder and inspiration to all men of all nations."

We are so proud of him that I could go on and on. The more Shoji learned English during his stay and talked about his background, the deeper our bonding grew. He was becoming Americanized very quickly, enough so that he felt comfortable to share his private thoughts and ideas with us. We savored these personal conversations as we came to know more of his character, especially his struggle with his traditional Japanese heritage.

Shoji was brought up on the island of Kyushu, the most conservative area in Japan. During his two years with us, he began to question many aspects of his culture.

Shoji's disciplined upbringing began when he was little. He explained that he had been studying karate with a teacher who was very rough. Sometimes, the teacher would beat him up so badly he could not go to school! As a result, Shoji was not afraid to fight. This was not true of his older brother, who shied away from physical confrontations. One day, when Shoji was in the third grade, he went to his brother's school and fought all of the sixth graders who had been picking on him!

His father also believed in tough love and would insist that Shoji put on armor and then fence with bamboo poles wrapped in leather. His father would also beat him across the arms and ribs. Once, he even forced Shoji out of the house for a few days because he was displeased with him. When I asked Shoji if he would cry during any of this cruel treatment, he said no. I certainly could relate to his difficult childhood, and our bonding strengthened.

Shoji also won my heart when he told us about helping his mother in the kitchen, despite his father's stern objection that "Japanese men do not do women's work."

"My mother was tired and had a lot of work to do," Shoji explained simply.

Whenever he was at our house, Shoji insisted on washing the dishes. One day, when he was standing at the sink, I put my arm around his waist and thanked him. I felt him stiffen and asked why. He explained that in Japan, there is no touching between boys and their mothers or grandmothers after they are no longer babies. This custom had been strictly followed in his home. However, he said that he wanted to learn to accept our demonstrations of love, because he admired American ways. Eventually, our greetings and farewells became warmer and more spontaneous.

Another aspect of Shoji's relationship with his family surfaced when we learned about his love of art: watercolors, woodcarvings, and poetry. In fact, Shoji had won first prize for one of his poems when he was in high school. His uncle, his mother's brother, had encouraged him to enjoy all of these activities, but his father was very displeased and forced him to stop spending time with these "useless" endeavors. Nevertheless, Shoji still had a love for music when he was with us, and when the students at St. Paul's Seminary gave him a guitar after he worked with them on a project, he quickly learned to play. He was particularly fond of songs by the folk trio Peter, Paul and Mary, and he played them all.

Ross and I treasured our time with Shoji. Once, when I was discussing Shoji with a psychologist friend, telling her how we had bonded despite our different ages and cultures, she volunteered to administer the Allport, Vernon, Lindzey Studies of Values test to all three of us. That was in September of 1969. After we completed the test, my friend recorded the results on a Profile of Values chart. The lines on the graph were almost identical for the three of us, whether below or above the median, for all values.

"Look at how far the three of you are above the median on social values," she pointed out, "and how far below the median you all are on economic values. These similar scores for all values explain why you three are so close, despite the difference in your cultures."

I was and still am fascinated by the results of this test, because Shoji's very conservative culture was the opposite of the liberal one he had encountered with us. Indeed, the graph of our results adds very interesting information for my ongoing debate on nature versus nurture!

After two years, it was time for Shoji to leave. We missed him very much when he returned to Kyushu. Although his postcards kept us informed of his life, we could not talk to him very often, because phone calls were so expensive. Shortly after he left, he sent us a photo album with pictures he had taken of people in Pearl City. The inscription read,

"To Mr. And Mrs. Ross Snyder, who taught me love." We were deeply touched.

Shoji was now attending Oita University in Kyushu, and he needed to write a thesis for his degree, similar to that for a Master's Degree in this country. Shoji had completed his other course work before he volunteered for the VTA program. He chose to write about his experiences with children of migrant workers at the South County Neighborhood Center; however, his superiors at the university decided that he should write about John Steinbeck's *Grapes of Wrath* instead. Shoji explained that he would rather write about his own experiences with migrant workers, but his wish was denied. He was so discouraged about his inability to pursue his passion that he wanted to drop all work on his thesis, but we urged him to stick it out and get his degree, which he did.

There were other situations at home that frustrated Shoji. For one, his father had picked out a bride for him; Shoji wanted to pick out his own wife and refused his father's choice. Also, his father wanted to get him a political appointment in Kyushu, but Shoji did not want that kind of a profession. Indeed, Shoji did not fit back into his former life. He had even joined a Unitarian group that met at the American Embassy, ignoring Shintoism, the religion of his family.

In November of 1971, more than a year after Shoji had left us, we received a long letter, in which he wrote, "I really miss you! And I wish I could have someone like you around me here.... I'm working at an orphanage in Tokyo as a janitor, the work itself is somewhat painful, not only physically but also spiritually.... I dream of the day when I can visit you.... I wish the day will come soon."

Shortly after getting this letter, we received a small book, filled with pictures of the children at the orphanage. The inscription read, "To my number one Mommy and Daddy, with deepest affection."

As flattered as we were by the outpouring of Shoji's feelings, we could tell how unhappy he was; and we were worried. He wrote that he was spending a lot of time in the mountains of Japan, meditating, and we hoped that he would find contentment.

A few more years went by as Shoji pondered his future. Then, in the summer of 1974, he wrote to say that he was coming to visit us. We were elated!

His first night with us, I gave him his guitar, which I had been saving for four years. He was surprised that we had not given it away, as he had instructed when he left. He began to play "Day Is Done," my favorite of Peter, Paul and Mary's songs. Shoji looked directly at me and smiled.

After he had been here for two weeks, he came down to breakfast one morning and startled us by asking, "How long would it take you to adopt me?"

"Are you serious?" I asked, my heart beating rapidly because I was afraid that I had not heard him correctly.

He said that he was very serious and had come back just to ask us to adopt him. "I'm a stranger in my own home and in my own country," he said. "I belong to this family and to this country."

We were thrilled! Then we thought of his biological parents. Had they agreed to this? Shoji explained that his mother was very understanding and wanted him to be happy. In fact, she made beautiful matching kimonos for the three of us after we adopted Shoji. On the other hand, Mr. Oue had felt humiliated and angry. Fate was on Shoji's side, however, because he was only the second son, so his father eventually agreed. If Shoji had been the firstborn, he would have been obligated to live as his father dictated. As it was, Shoji planned to keep contact with his biological parents and brother.

Ross and I immediately made an appointment with our attorney to begin the adoption proceedings. In two weeks, Shoji was Shoji Oue Snyder!

Shoji was determined to make us proud of him. He split his time between Japan and the United States as an international marketing and research analyst. Among his clients were all the major airlines that flew into Japan. For example, he helped Boeing arrange sales of planes to different airlines, and he also assisted Delta in their negotiations with Japan when they began to fly into that country.

Even though we kept in constant contact with each other, we had to be satisfied with only one or two visits a year, in addition to special birthdays and other occasions.

Whenever Shoji came home, he would have a special gift for Ross and me. It might be an exotic statuette from Sri Lanka, a watch, or a beautiful necklace. Once, he remarked that I drank only instant coffee.

I explained that I was the only coffee drinker in the house, and it was too much trouble to make a pot of coffee just for me.

A few days later, he came home with a small coffee grinder and a machine for making a single cup of coffee. He made a cup for me and then stood anxiously waiting to see if it was to my liking.

"It's a little strong,' I said.

The next time he made coffee for me, I commented that it was a little weak.

The third time I happily exclaimed, feeling somewhat like Goldilocks, "It's just right; it's delicious!"

With that, he smiled and said quite seriously, "Now what you do is take thirty-six beans and grind them. Don't touch the setting; I have it on three...."

Of course, I do not count thirty-six beans each time I make coffee, but I think of him and how meticulous he was in trying to please me. That was our son!

He found a girl he loved, Hatsue, and they moved in together. He often brought her to visit us. We loved her and thought of her as a daughter-in-law.

I wrote the following poem for our new son:

Happiness

Happiness
Is a feeling
That swells inside
Until the pressure
Forces tears
From the eyes.

THE BRIGIDIO
EDUARDO "EDDIE"
CABRERA CASE

The following events were the result of my work with the South County Neighborhood Center. On Saturday morning, March 12, 1973, two men knocked on my door, pleading for help. I recognized the younger man as Nick Moreno, who at one time had come to SCNC for help in finding employment. The older man introduced himself as Nick's father-in-law, Juan Cabrera.

"Nick said that you could help us," he said simply.

A Delray Beach policeman had shot and killed Cabrera's sixteen-year-old son, Eddie, the previous night. Cabrera wanted help in getting a doctor to examine his son's body before the medical examiner performed an autopsy. According to the officers, the youth was running from the police when he was shot by accident. Juan did not believe the police version, however, because his son was a good boy who had never gotten into any serious trouble.

I called Dr. James Moseley, a close friend and our family doctor in Boca Raton, who agreed to go to Bethesda Hospital to observe the autopsy. He confirmed the path of the bullet as Dr. Cuevas, the assistant medical examiner, described it. Dr. Cuevas said the bullet entered the right elbow at a forty-five-degree angle, exited below the elbow, then entered the side, and went through the heart and lung. According to Dr. Cuevas, one bullet caused all three wounds. Dr. Mosely told me that in order for this to happen, the right arm must have been contorted, bent back and out, for the bullet to go into and out of the upper arm, into and out of the lower arm, then into the side and through the heart and lung.

I decided that I needed to talk to some witnesses as soon as possible. People I interviewed generally agreed about the events before the shooting. Eddie was sitting on the hood of his boss's car, waiting for a ride home. He worked for Joe Rolle in his auto parts store. It had been Friday night, and the street and parking lot were crowded.

Rolle was at the "little green house in the neighborhood" where gambling took place. That night, a raid occurred. The crowd scattered when police cars arrived with lights flashing. A woman standing near Eddie shouted at him to run. Eddie jumped off the car and took off. While other officers stormed the house, one chased Eddie west in the dark between two houses. From that point, there are two versions of what occurred.

According to the police version, the officer chased Eddie through a weed-filled alley and around the corner of a house. This is where the officer collided with the boy, causing his gun to accidentally discharge. I walked from the parking lot where Eddie had been waiting for his boss to the area between the two houses where the body had fallen. The spot was in the middle of an unpaved but smooth driveway, not at the corner of the house. There was nothing in evidence that could have caused the officer to trip or lose his footing. While I was interviewing the woman who lived next door, a young boy kept pulling on my skirt.

"Miss, I heard the shots."

Shots? More than one? I quickly asked him exactly what he heard.

"It was Bang! Bang! Like that," he said.

I found four adult witnesses who also heard two quick shots. One woman said she had been worried about policemen running through the area, chasing men from the pool room or bars with their guns drawn, in utter disregard for the safety of the black people in the community. Then I found two more very important witnesses, two men who saw the officer, Edwin Rozier, holding Eddie by the elbow, with his gun drawn. He was walking Eddie back east off the pavement to the shoulder of the road.

One of the men said, "Maybe two or three minutes later, we drove back to the spot and were told that Eddie had been shot resisting arrest.

I couldn't believe that, because Eddie was standing quietly when I saw him."

As a result of the testimony of all the witnesses, I concluded that the officer had walked Eddie back east to the dark driveway, some fifteen feet from the street, where he shot and killed the boy.

There was no formal police investigation by the Delray Police Department, so I was never able to learn whether Rozier's gun had been checked to determine how many shots had been fired. On April 5, 1973, the grand jury issued its findings, exonerating the officer by ruling that the shooting was "excusable homicide." I was as convinced as Eddie's father that his son had been murdered.

Unable to get justice in criminal court, Juan Cabrera decided to sue in civil court. He used an attorney from Miami, and on July 31, 1975, the city of Delray Beach settled the suit out of court, awarding Cabrera $100,000. Unfortunately, nothing was ever done about Edwin Rozier's role in the shooting.

Getting a Degree

Before I met Ross, when I was thirty years old, I took the General Education Development Test and got a high school equivalency diploma (GED). Once we moved to Florida, I started to take college courses at night. Progress was slow, because I was working at a variety of jobs. Ross convinced me to quit work and go to school full time. I finished my first two years of college at Brevard Junior College in Cocoa, Florida. Then we moved south so I could attend Florida Atlantic University in Boca Raton. Ross took the job of university planner in July of 1964. I enrolled in the university the following fall.

No longer painfully shy, I chose government and politics, because I wanted to work in an area that would be challenging and that would contribute in some way to solving many of the social problems of our times. My experiences as an abused child had made me stronger—more focused and compassionate. Now I wanted to help others conquer forces working against them. Sometimes I felt overwhelmed by the racism, cruelty, greed, and poverty in the world.

When I enrolled as a political science major at Florida Atlantic University in 1964, Dr. John DeGrove, then chair of the department, told me that he knew of our successful fight to defeat the Port Authority bill and get a new airport going. (Orlando International Airport had just opened.) He was impressed that such a small number of people could win despite such overwhelming odds, and I was flattered that he recognized our accomplishment.

When I graduated with a BA in government and politics in December of 1965, I decided that the only way to approach problems I had noticed that weren't being addressed successfully was by dealing with them one at a time in my own community. When I became a reporter for the *Fort Lauderdale News*, I knew that I would have that chance.

INVESTIGATIVE
REPORTING

I was thrilled to be a reporter on the *Fort Lauderdale News*. My editor, Bare Bowman, understood and encouraged me in my investigative reporting and community activities. During the next four years, I wrote about the desperate working and living conditions of migrant workers, about witnessing racial discrimination and police brutality. I also wrote about the abuses in mental hospitals. There was never a lack of good stories, but they had to be sandwiched in between routine stories, like city council, county commission, and school board meetings.

Then Bare was moved to another desk, and everything changed. I had a new editor, who rewrote my stories until the meaning was often lost or changed. Finally, I quit and took a year off to help establish a juvenile delinquency prevention program at the South County Neighborhood Center. When I went back to reporting, this time at the *Boca Raton News*, the editor, Davis "Buzz" Merritt, was of the same school of thought as Bare. During the next three years, I received eight awards for my writing about and working on community problems. Among them were the Florida Education Association School Bell Award, the National Mental Health Association's Mental Health Bell Award, and the Award for Excellence in Public Service from the Florida Society of Newspaper Editors.

On December 2, 1973, I began my eleven-part series on the South Florida State [Mental] Hospital, where the doctor-patient ratio was one to 135. The feeling of shock and revulsion I experienced the first time I saw the maximum-security ward at South Florida State Hospital was followed immediately by a vow to do something about it. What follow are excerpts from that series.

I had been told that Washington Ward was a hellhole. It was one of four security wards in Florida State Hospital, used primarily for court hold patients—those who had not had their trials yet because they were deemed incompetent to stand trial. The idea was that the care at the hospital would improve their mental states so that they could stand trial. The men in Washington Ward were there because they were sick, but everything about the place spelled prisoner instead of patient. From everything I learned, I could understand how someone who was not mentally ill when he came in became mentally ill while staying there.

Patients were held in caged cells without toilet or water facilities. The barber chair in the otherwise empty room next to the cells even reminded me of an electric chair in a prison. The American Civil Liberties Union (ACLU) was threatening suit because patients were treated like prisoners, living in caged areas that seemed identical to those found in medieval prisons and dilapidated zoos.

In my mind's eye, I imagined dogs on the filthy mattresses on the cold concrete floors of those cells instead of humans. However, I doubted that humane societies would permit their animals to be treated in such a way. These humans were constantly beaten up and tied up illegally.

For years, it had been easier for patients to escape than for reporters to get in. But my first visit to the hospital verified everything I had been told. When a mother of one of the inmates, Jimmy, contacted me about her son's treatment in Washington Ward, I managed to get a visitor's pass, posing as a social worker. I stood behind her as she signed in on her next visit to her son. I asked the staff questions that a social worker would ask, such as whether Jimmy was improving. Then I signed in as Alice Snyder, Alice being my middle name. I am certain that when the staff saw a nicely dressed white woman with a briefcase, accompanying the working class black woman whose son was in Washington Ward for the criminally insane, they concluded that I was a social worker.

Once inside Washington Ward, I continued playing the role of a social worker, discussing Jimmy's condition with the staff. No one was paying attention to the inmates, so I was able to wander over to other cells. I spoke to a teenager lying on the floor.

"Where do you go to the toilet"? I asked.

"I defecate on a paper plate and urinate in a paper cup," he answered.

I turned to an aide who was hovering nearby and asked, "Is that true?"

"Unfortunately, it is," he responded, looking around to make sure no one was near enough to hear him.

I sensed a sympathetic tone in his voice and decided to take a chance. Making sure that we were alone, I lowered my voice.

"Look, I'm going to trust you. I'm not a social worker. I'm a reporter for the *Boca Raton News*, investigating conditions here."

"Thank God," he replied with feeling. "It's about time someone did. I'll help you in any way I can."

That was the beginning of my relationship with Jon, who gave me invaluable information for my series. Using an inside informer was my favorite way to work. Luck certainly played a part in this situation, because it was Jon and not an unsympathetic aide who happened to be near me, but I took a risk and did not let the luck slip away. This combination of good fortune and my intuition served me well then and in my future as a private investigator.

Jon encouraged other patients to call me collect, write to me, or hand me notes on my visits as a social worker. Although visitors were not permitted to carry purses or anything into the building, I was able to smuggle a camera under my loose-fitting blouses. When no staff was around, I undid one button and took pictures, which were published with the article.

As I wrote the series of articles, I shared everything I learned with O. J. Keller, then state director of Health and Rehabilitative Services (now known as the Department of Children and Families). He appointed a blue-ribbon committee to investigate allegations against the hospital. Although the poor conditions at Washington Ward were common knowledge among officials in Broward and Dade counties, I was the first person to document everything.

Now Keller had the information he needed to make some changes. On December 21, 1973, Keller announced that Dr. Rufus M. Vaughn would replace Richard H. Parks as superintendent of the South Florida State Hospital. A few days later, I wrote in the "Reporter's Notebook" section of my paper that I was often asked the question, "What can one person do?" I responded with, "I know that one person can do a lot, particularly if that one person enlists others who are also interested in the problem to be tackled."

And indeed, Dr. Vaughn cleaned up the mess at the hospital. Not long after Park's departure, Dr. William Rogers, director of the State Division of Mental Health, was forced to retire.

The Johnnie Davenport, Jr. Case

While I was still active at the South County Neighborhood Center and also a full-time reporter at the *Boca Raton News*, I started writing a six-part series called "The Death of Johnnie Davenport," which began in December of 1972. I was working under the outstanding Davis "Buzz" Merritt. He had great confidence in me and gave me the go-ahead when I told him about the Davenport case.

The morning of May 14, 1968, Johnnie Davenport was booked into the Boca Raton jail on a traffic ticket. Two hours later, he was found dead. Police said that he hanged himself from the upper bunk with his undershirt. (The cause of death on the death certificate was misspelled: "asphiyxiation.") No one who knew Johnnie believed that this young black man would take his own life. The thirty-one year-old husband and father, who worked two full-time jobs and one part-time job to support his family, was making plans to add on to his house and buy a second car.

"The idea that Johnnie, who served three years in the army as a medical technician, would kill himself over a traffic ticket is ridiculous," a close friend of Johnnie's told me. "If he was going to commit suicide, why would he call his wife after his arrest and ask her to come bail him out?"

I followed the story as Davenport's wife filed a complaint with the Civil Rights Division of the U.S. Department of Justice and retained Alcee Hastings, then in private practice and now a U.S. Representative, to represent her. Hastings was able to get the body exhumed for a second autopsy, which unfortunately corroborated the original medical examiner's view that the cause of death was a suicide. Reluctantly, Hastings backed off from filing a lawsuit on Mrs. Davenport's behalf, although the case stuck with him and "tugged at his heart," he told me thirty years later.

I would not drop the case, however. When Buzz said I could do a six-part series four years later, I believed that once I revealed all the evidence I had collected, the case would be reopened. For example, Mose Turner, who had been a janitor at the jail and had alerted officers when he found Davenport's body, told me that there was blood splattered on the floor outside and inside Davenport's cell. Davenport, who was shirtless, had a T-shirt around his neck, but Turner said that it hung loosely and was not knotted. Most important, Davenport's body was in a sitting position on the lower bunk, with his feet on the floor. Turner told me that he did not know what happened after he alerted officers about Davenport.

"I was told I wasn't needed back there," he said.

Turner was fired a few months later for "not doing his job satisfactorily."

Once it became clear that I was working on the series for the newspaper, Boca Raton Police Chief Charles McCutcheon, who had been assistant police chief at the time of Davenport's death, asked for a grand jury investigation. I was hopeful that the truth would be revealed.

For one, the ambulance driver from the Boca Raton Community Hospital, where the body was taken, said that the corpse had an IBM maintenance uniform on, which was buttoned to the top. This contradicted Mose Turner's testimony that the body was shirtless. The driver, who was interviewed by a private investigator hired by the Davenport family and friends soon after Johnnie's death, reportedly found it strange that a man would take off his undershirt to hang himself, then put his uniform back on and button it to up to his neck. Also, he noticed that the victim still had his belt on and wondered why he had not used the belt to hang himself.

Officers contended that Davenport was shouting and going berserk in his cell, which was denied by other witnesses.

Police officer Emery Brooks, who saw Davenport when he was brought in, said, "He made a statement that he would beat them in court, but he was not loud or hostile," Brooks said.

There were also numerous inconsistencies in statements by the officers on duty that morning—there were thirteen of them—about the position of the body. Furthermore, officers reported that the prisoner in the next cell told police that he heard a choking sound coming from Davenport's cell. When I interviewed him, though, that same prisoner denied ever hearing the noise or saying that he heard the noise.

Then there was a conversation I had with the chief of police, Hugh Brown, shortly after Davenport's death. He lectured me for over half an hour.

"You know, I know everything that goes on in this town, whether in schools, the churches, but I don't always use that information," he told me.

Since I had just started the South County Neighborhood Center in the Unitarian Universalist Church near the police station, I thought he was indirectly threatening me. Something in his voice alerted me to his real intent.

"You must remember, Chief Brown, that reporters frequently know a lot about what is going on in a town, but they don't always use the information," I replied.

He then told me that that thin blue line is our best defense against Communism, to which I replied that an informed public was our best defense, whether against Communism or something that was happening in the community.

Four and a half years later, when the grand jury convened in January of 1973, I was the only witness called to testify. The investigator hired by the prosecutor for the grand jury, T. D. Walker, had not even interviewed most of the witnesses whose names I had given him. Mose Turner had been only partially interviewed before the investigator ran out of tape.

At the time I went before the grand jury, I had fifty items I wanted to bring to their attention. Much to my frustration, Palm Beach County State Attorney David Bludworth did not let me get back to my list after the first four or five times. This was not a fact-finding hearing; it was a trial, and I felt as if I were the defendant.

For example, Bludworth asked if Alcee Hastings, Mrs. Davenport's former lawyer, was paying me to do the investigation all these years.

There were also constant admonitions by Bludworth, such as "Let's move along," that prevented me from exploring even those areas I got an opportunity to mention. Bludworth also told the grand jury that I was writing a book about Johnnie Davenport at the time, which I was not. The hearing lasted only thirty minutes,

I believe that the thrust of that grand jury investigation, as I felt about Walker's investigation, was to divert attention from serious questions about Davenport's death to raise doubts about my credibility and motives. This was my first experience in how a grand jury can be misled and manipulated by the prosecutor, who makes the decision about what evidence and what witnesses will be presented. Predictably, the grand jury's finding was that Davenport committed suicide.

Twenty-six years later, in January of 1999, Robert McCabe, a *Sun Sentinel* news reporter, brought a thirty-nine-year-old black man to see me. He was Fred Davenport, the son of Johnnie Davenport, who had been nine years old when his father died. He had been a Broward County Sheriff's officer since 1988. It was quite an emotional meeting for both of us. I was happy to tell Fred why I was so certain that his father had not committed suicide, and Fred finally had information he had never known, because his family refused to discuss the case. McCabe wrote a story for the *Sun Sentinel* titled "The education of Sgt. Davenport: A decorated cop's 30-year struggle to understand his father's death in the custody of the police." It was published January 24, 1999.

After thirty-seven years, I am still hopeful that the murderer or murderers of Johnnie Davenport will be brought to justice. There is no statute of limitations on murder. The beauty of this fact is that forensic technology has improved so much over the years that people working on cold case files can uncover the truth.

FLORIDA RURAL
LEGAL SERVICES

When Buzz was promoted to the *Miami Herald*'s Washington Bureau, we had a series of new editors, the latest being Max Veale. When I returned from accepting my eighth award, he and his boss, Tom Schumacher, fired me.

I had been expecting this, because Veale had been spreading the news that I was not a good writer and that he had been trying to teach me. When I had told him about my seventh award, the Stanley Milledge Award "for the individual making the most significant contribution to the cause of civil liberties in Florida 1974," he did not even put an item in the newspaper. The situation had become so strained at work that I had vowed to find another job after receiving the Mental Health Bell Award, but I never had the chance.

I believe that Veale was jealous of my success, although he said he fired me because he did not want his reporters involved in the community. I was outraged, and I did not go "gentle into that dark night." I bought a display ad in the newspaper to tell my readers what had happened and filed an age discrimination complaint with the Office of Equal Opportunity. The federal investigator of my complaint thoroughly investigated the situation and agreed that Veale was jealous of me. I felt vindicated.

Being fired was no surprise, but losing my job before I had found another one was devastating. I was the sole breadwinner at that time. Ross had developed a severe allergy to cigarette smoke a few months earlier and was forced to give up his job in an engineering office where everyone smoked. Veale and Schumacher both knew this. It was a rough time. We even applied for food stamps before I found a job.

A few months after I was fired, I went to work as a paralegal for Florida Rural Legal Services. This organization had received a grant for emergency food and medical services for migrant workers. These people had problems, ranging from language difficulties to lack of information about where they could receive help. In addition, we also served other poor people in the area, whose needs were the same. Our clients had too many overwhelming problems for our small staff to handle, so I started a full-time volunteer program to assist us. A case history of one of my migrant clients illustrates what we faced in our office every day.

Mr. Hall was a slight, black man who looked much older that the sixty-four years he claimed. His bent posture and knobby hands were indicative of his many years of hard work. He came to our office for help in getting emergency food. He needed to get recertified for food stamps after he had been robbed of them the month before. He still had to wait another week.

The supervisor told me that she would need proof that Mr. Hall had reported the theft to the police department. Since there was a charge for a police report—Mr. Hall had no money whatsoever—I called the police department and asked if he could get a free copy. They agreed as long as I would write a referral, which I did.

After taking care of the food stamp arrangements, I learned in conversation with Mr. Hall that he was born in Georgia. He had not attended school, so he could not read or write. His wife, nine children, and twelve grandchildren lived in Bainbridge, Georgia. He had been coming to Florida in the winter to work in the vegetable fields since 1939, because he could make more money here than he could in Georgia. He said that he always came down at the beginning of the season, sent his money back home, and then returned when the season ended in spring.

However, this season Mr. Hall had not been able to get much work, because his eyesight was so poor that he had to feel for the peppers he was to pick. The crew leader would not let him work every day, because he was too slow. An occasional day's picking enabled him to pay fifteen dollars a week for the tiny room he was renting. Three months earlier, he had been living at Fred's Motel on U.S. 441, a trashy place where migrant workers were charged exorbitant rent and were often victims of crime. While he was staying there, he had been robbed of everything in his pocket, including the keys to his suitcase. Soon after, he had moved into town, because he was afraid.

Before he came to Florida Rural Legal Services, Mr. Hall had gone to West Palm Beach to sign up for Social Security. The person in charge told him that he did not have enough quarters of earned income to qualify. Actually, the form they gave him showed zero quarters. I was not surprised, because I knew that the crew leaders who hired migrant workers frequently did not pay Social Security for them.

Mr. Hall said that his crew leader had told him and seventy other workers that he had been taking a dollar a day from their wages for Social Security! Mr. Hall was desperate. He was two months behind on his rent and had no food.

To make matters worse, he did not have his birth certificate with him to verify his age, because he had not been able to get his suitcases open since he was robbed. I called a local locksmith and talked him into opening the suitcases and making new keys for them. As soon as the locksmith finished, Mr. Hall handed me an envelope containing a number of well-worn papers. Included was a folded and torn census report proving that he had been born four years earlier than he had told me, which meant that he was sixty-eight. Now he could apply for Aid to the Aged—and could have done so three years earlier!

I took him to the Social Security office and assisted him in applying for his SSI benefits. He would soon be receiving $146 a month for the rest of his life, and he could earn up to sixty-five dollars a month without having to report it. I wrote a letter to the Social Security office in Bainbridge, explaining everything. I then made arrangements for Mr. Hall to get an eye examination paid for by the Bureau of the Blind. When he had his prescription, Lions Industries paid for his glasses. Finally, a very grateful Mr. Hall was ready to return to Bainbridge.

It is necessary to multiply Mr. Hall by the thousands, or even the hundreds of thousands, to understand the overwhelming problems we faced. My social conscience was working overtime. However, I had to decide what I could realistically do to change bigotry, greed, and corruption. I decided that I could not take on all the big problems. Rather, I could begin with the small problems and work up to the big ones.

For example, in what I call the Termite Approach, one begins with a little crevice and begins chewing away. It is not always possible to bring the whole building down, but I can make a lot of progress before anyone realizes what is happening. I also have The Skunk Approach when the problem calls for quick action. In these cases, I raise as much stink as I can by getting many other people joining the cause. Sometimes I use one approach or the other, sometimes both—whatever it takes. When people say, "You can't fight city hall," I disagree, because I have done it.

Tigers

My aunt loved butterflies.
She would watch them play
Outside her window
And marvel at their delicate beauty.

My aunt hated corruption
And violence.
A report of police brutality
Would make her furious.

She would call officials,
Write letters to the editor,
Even picket.
But she loved butterflies,
Especially tiger butterflies.

REFLECTIONS ON MY MOTHER

For two years, I worked as a paralegal for Florida Legal Services while deciding what direction to take with my professional life. I was fifty-five years old and had no intention of retiring. Rather, I wanted a career in which I could utilize my investigative skills and experience and not be at the mercy of an insensitive boss. Ross suggested that I start a private investigative agency. It was the answer to my dilemma. On November 27, 1976, my fifty-sixth birthday, I opened the office in a wing of our house.

It was a very emotional time for me, because a few months earlier, my Mama had died from cancer. She had been failing and rallying for weeks. When Juanita called to say that she was weaker and the pain was getting worse, I flew home. I had dreamed about Mama two nights before. It was a vivid dream, in color. There was no sign of the wheelchair to which Mama had been confined so many years after a stroke. Instead, she walked into a room where a hearing of some kind was underway. She was straight-backed, and her walk was purposeful. Only the nightgown and robe, familiar attire for so long, served as a reminder that she was an invalid. I puzzled over the dream the next morning; when Juanita called, I wondered uneasily if it had been a premonition.

During my flight, a feeling of tragedy overwhelmed me, not for her impending death, but for her life. My earliest recollections were of Mama cooking, cleaning, carrying wood into the kitchen to burn in the kitchen range, bending over a washboard, ironing clothes with a flatiron that had been heated on the stove, milking cows, and working in the fields with the hired hands. I remembered the headaches she suffered.

Sometimes they were so severe that she would lie down with a cold cloth over her eyes. Sometimes, if she had too much work to do, she would tie a wet cloth around her temples and continue with her chores.

As we grew up, we tried to get her to stand up to Daddy, to stop letting him browbeat her. "You don't have to put up with it, Mama," we would tell her angrily, but she would just change the subject. We realized that when the children were young, she had no place to go if she had to leave her husband, but after all the children were grown, we could not understand why she would not be more independent.

Mama had enjoyed life so much more after Daddy died. She took delight in the simplest pleasures in a way we had never seen her do when he was alive. Her girlish laughter, her enjoyment of harmless practical jokes and of little surprises had been stifled for fifty-five years.

He died of a massive heart attack when he was eighty. It was quick. One minute, Daddy was talking on the phone. The next, my oldest brother heard a sigh, looked around, and saw the telephone sliding down Daddy's shoulder.

At the insistence of the family a few years earlier, Daddy had made a will, but he had not picked out a burial plot. Mama's only request was that my brothers pick a spot that would not be muddy when it rained. They chose the highest point in the cemetery. After the funeral, as we left the cemetery, I felt overwhelmed by sadness—not because of Daddy's death, but because of the wasted years, because of his destructiveness to Mama and me.

At the dinner after the funeral, Mama sat in her wheelchair at the head of the table, surrounded by her six children and their families. She smiled as she watched her grandchildren playing.

During a lull, I said, "Mama, you're the head of the family now. Give us an order."

Mama smiled but said nothing. Daddy had made all of her decisions. Now we wanted her to have a chance.

"Go ahead, practice," we teased.

"Why start now?" she asked with a chuckle.

We paused a short while and changed the topic.

When I arrived home for the last week of her life, I learned about an incident during her first year of marriage to my father. She was fifteen when she married and knew nothing about cooking or housekeeping.

She said, "I baked some biscuits, and he complained that they were too hard, so I threw one at him."

There was a long pause. Finally, I asked, "What did he do?"

"He hit me with his fist," she answered softly.

Suddenly, I understood why she was so terrified of this husband who was ten years her senior. He had conquered her with that one blow. It must have been frustrating for him when he could not control me, no matter how many times he hit me.

When she told us the story, I finally understood why Mama would plead with Daddy to stop beating me and then become silent as soon as he raised his fist and told her to shut up. I decided then that I would help other victims like Mama and later became a founding member of Aid to Victims of Domestic Assault.

That last week, we took turns sitting with her, rotating shifts so we could all get some sleep. She was able to sit up and visit with us until the last few days. The teenage grandchildren also took turns. I was thankful that she took her last breath in my arms when it was my turn. I was also thankful that I could return to Florida and start a new career after letting go of Mama. I still grieve more for her life than for her death.

LIFE AS A P.I.

I was only the second woman in Florida to obtain a private investigator's license and own an agency. Just about every P.I. was a former law enforcement officer, which explains the lack of women in the profession. I had numerous advantages, being a gray-haired and overweight woman. I could do the female version of Tim Conway's shuffling old man and go almost anywhere and get away with anything.

"I guess I got the address mixed up," I would respond if someone stopped me; or if I were watching a building, I'd explain, "I'm waiting for my daughter to pick me up," or "My feet got tired, so I thought I would just sit here and rest a while."

Most people think in stereotypes, so a little old lady out in the field, wearing a floppy hat and sensible shoes, carrying binoculars and a bird book, is a bird watcher. If I looked up in the trees and then flipped pages in the bird book, I could also look across the canal without arousing suspicion. I once served a subpoena on a man who had been avoiding the sheriff's process-server for six months. As an older woman with nothing in my hands, I posed no threat when I knocked on his door. When he opened up, I pulled the papers out of my bra and served him!

I often took advantage of the tendency for people to stereotype others. For example, when I trained interns in my field, I told them not to wear any jewelry and not to overdress. I stressed that they should wear ordinary clothing that was clean and neat, so they would not intimidate possible witnesses with their attire.

Most importantly, I told them not to intimidate witnesses with their demeanor. Everyone should be treated with dignity and respect. For instance, I usually begin an interview with a general positive statement, such as, "What a beautiful hibiscus tree you have in your yard" or "What a cute dog...." Then I say something like, "By the way, I'm

75

Virginia Snyder, a private investigator, and I've been hired by attorney [so and so] to find out about a suspected child molester. I'd like to get at the truth, and I'm hoping you can help me." If the individual was helpful in any way, I would follow up with a thank-you, either a note or phone call. That was the best way I found to develop a network of people who trusted me.

My earlier work as an investigative reporter for many years helped me establish my new business, because I had made so many contacts in the South Florida area. My practice took off as soon as I opened my agency. Several years later, my husband, Ross, and my nephew, Wayne Campbell, joined me. Wayne was able to use the latest technology available in our searches and investigations, which made the agency even more successful.

People have often wondered how I had the time and energy to pursue my profession. The key was Ross, who has always been my greatest supporter and helper. He did all the grocery shopping, cooking, and most of the laundry for us. In doing so, he freed me from the stress and time of running a household, so that I could devote myself primarily to helping my clients. He did it, he always said, out of love for me and admiration for my work.

Many people ask how I could handle so many murder cases without being afraid for my own life or without becoming totally despondent when an innocent person was convicted. I answer that I do not spend my days contemplating the darkest deeds of other people. I am fully aware of and sensitive to the human condition—whatever it may be. On a personal level, I had suffered from my father's darkest deeds during my entire childhood, yet I had stood up to him; and I had emerged a stronger woman.

My social conscience was part of me for as long as I can remember, and it continued to grow as I matured. As a result, I felt compelled to improve and correct whatever I could. However, if my client was not saved from death row, or if an innocent person remained in prison in spite of everything I had done, I did not let it get me down. I put the case in the back of my mind and went on to the next one. I did not forget, however; I just stopped for the time being. If and when there was a new development, or if I learned about some possibility of reopening a case, I did it. I did everything I could; that way, I was not torn by guilt or self-reproach. Lack of success has never conquered me.

PROFESSIONAL CRONYISM AND THE MARK HERMAN CASE

Professional cronyism subverts the ideals of justice in our democracy. Whether it is court officials protecting court officials, police officers protecting police officers, or doctors protecting doctors, the average citizen is the loser.

For example, one of my clients, a police officer in Delray Beach, filed an accurate report of a racial incident between blacks and the police, despite repeated pressure on him to change his report. He was told by his superiors, "You're letting your buddies down."

This same officer was soon transferred out of his unit and given a 5 percent pay cut. The police chief insisted that the transfer and cut in pay had nothing to do with the above report; it was just that the other officers did not want to work with him. The police chief had chosen not to enforce laws that would have protected the victimized officer from his peers, a situation that is all too common. The other victims were the poor blacks in the precinct, which is also all too common.

On another occasion, a highly respected medical doctor urged me to investigate and expose a surgeon who was doing unnecessary surgery (we later learned) to support his drug habit. Both doctors were on the staff of the same hospital.

"Why doesn't the hospital's own committee on personnel take action to stop him? I asked.

"Everyone's afraid of getting sued," the doctor replied.

This surgeon later left the state and was busted on drug-related charges. In the meantime, the hospital allowed him to victimize people by making them go through unnecessary surgery! There are plenty of laws on the books that would have protected the hospital had it investigated the doctor and subsequently taken him off the staff.

Here's an example of the worst kind of professional cronyism.

In 1976, Richard Kreusler, a wealthy oilman, was shot when he answered his front door. He survived a few days but was unable to identify his killer. Mark Herman, a handsome local karate expert and petty criminal, who was already in jail for an unrelated crime, was charged with Kreusler's murder. His mother believed that he was innocent of the murder and hired me to work with his attorney, Alphonso Sepe of Miami.

Within two weeks, I had developed information about the murder from witnesses who pointed directly to the killer, a hit man for a drug ring. I even learned where the murder weapon and shells had likely come from.

When I called to tell Sepe the exciting news, he was not in, so I told his secretary, "I think I know who murdered Richard Kreusler; it was Jake-the-Snake.'" This case was like an old mystery thriller: a wealthy Palm Beach victim, a handsome young defendant, lying witnesses, and three attorneys with conflicts of interest because they also represented the actual killer, whose nickname was straight from an old gangster movie!

"Oh, that's one of Mr. Sepe's clients," the secretary replied.

I lamented, "That will probably mean Mr. Sepe will have to withdraw from Herman's case."

There was a brief pause, then she said, "No, that won't be necessary. He has already withdrawn as attorney from Jake-the-Snake's case."

I accepted her explanation because I knew that Sepe was having health problems and had probably cut back on his workload. However, I became puzzled when I did not hear from Sepe for weeks. I had been sending my reports to his office, but I had the feeling he was not even reading them.

A few weeks after my initial call to Sepe's office, his secretary finally called me. "Mr. Sepe wants you to slow down on your investigation, because it looks like neither of you is going to get paid," she told me.

I told her that I would not slow down, that I would rather wait for my money than to stop in the middle of an investigation that was going so well. I did not tell her that I now knew something was wrong with

Sepe's reaction to my theory that Jake-the-Snake had killed Kreusler. After all, the best way to prove that one's client is innocent is to find the guilty party!

I hung up and called the Dade County Clerk's Office to learn if Sepe had withdrawn from Jake-the-Snake's case. The clerk checked the file and could find no evidence that he had withdrawn but did find that another attorney, Joseph Mincberg, had been assigned to Jake's case on the very day of my first call to Sepe's office. Not long after this conversation, I received a letter from Sepe, dismissing me from the case. Now I believed that Sepe's purpose in agreeing to be Mark's defense attorney was to protect Jake-the-Snake.

Mark was very upset when he learned of Sepe's actions and insisted that I be kept on the job. He had hired Sepe on the recommendation of a friend who was involved in drug dealing in West Palm Beach and who knew Sepe. I cautioned Mark about Sepe and his appeals lawyers, but Mark was naïve and chose to trust his friend and them. Sepe reluctantly agreed to keep me on the case but showed very little interest in my findings. When it came time for the trial, I made sure that all of the witnesses I found were on the witness list, but Sepe did not call a single one. He even discouraged Herman from taking the stand in his own defense.

State Attorney David Bludworth, who in my opinion wanted a conviction more than he wanted the truth, produced jailhouse snitches as his witnesses. One was a Mafia hit man already convicted of two murders and awaiting trial for a third. They testified that Herman had admitted to them that he committed the murder. One of the state's witnesses even produced a "confession" that he said Herman had written. In spite of my pleas and those of Mark and his mother, Sepe did not have the letter examined by a handwriting expert. Many years later, the letter was determined to be a forgery.

His trial, the first ever televised in South Florida, was shown on Channel 2 in 1997. It was obvious to many viewers who contacted me afterward that Mark was framed. It was also very obvious to many lawyers who watched the trial and who knew the reputation of the defense attorney that Mark was framed. Nevertheless, they would not come forward to challenge the powers that be.

In the meantime, I was vilified by those powers to the point that my business and reputation were affected—more importantly, to the point that my frustration and disappointment in my fellow man swelled to painful levels for six years. I understood that the average citizen would shy away from a confrontation with someone like a state's attorney, but I was very disappointed that so many people who worked in the judicial system would not come forward.

Mark was found guilty and sentenced to a mandatory twenty-five years for first-degree murder. The judge could have sentenced him to the electric chair, but he stated that, given the quality of the state's witnesses, he could not sentence Herman to death. In the following years, two other attorneys represented Herman on appeals and clemency hearings. Neither of these attorneys used the information I had gathered that pointed to the real possibility that Mark had been framed. Neither did they call witnesses who would have testified about who did the crime, who ordered it, and why. Both attorneys, Joseph Mincberg and Steve Johnson (the latter had called Mark and volunteered his services) also represented Jake-the-Snake. The appeal and the clemency were both denied.

I would not stop my attempts to free Herman. I contacted Governor Reubin Askew, who instructed Bludworth to investigate my findings and report back. Sepe's response to this, as reported in the *Miami Herald*, was that I was a dangerous woman and that he had never wanted me on the case.

Bludworth assigned the investigation to an assistant state's attorney, Joel Weissman, who proceeded to interview the people on my witness list. As Weissman and I waited outside the courtroom during Herman's appeal, he told me that his report would support my theory that Herman was framed. However, Joseph Mincberg never called Weissman to testify!

Although Bludworth had stated that he would make the report public, the investigation dragged on for months, until Askew had left office. Then Bludworth refused to release the report. It was now September of 1982. I decided to write a letter to the editor in the *Boca Raton News*, criticizing Bludworth for not releasing the report. It was printed on September 19. I stated in part:

> I am concerned, professionally, about the absence
> of a report that may have cleared my client. In the
> absence of any statement to the contrary, I feel my
> theory may have been confirmed....

And today, even though four of the State's witnesses have stated under oath, and publicly (even on ABC's *20/20*), that they lied, Bludworth has made no move to correct this miscarriage of justice. He is busy running for the U.S. Senate, and Mark Herman is still in prison.

Bludworth replied with a letter to the editor of the same newspaper, printed September 24. In part, he wrote:

I have a serious question about the responsibility of your newspaper to review factual basis for letters that reflect upon public officials. This should he particularly so since the writer of one letter, Virginia Snyder, has a history of being unreliable and misinformed....

I have been a prosecutor in this county since 1967. I, along with many other law enforcement agencies, have had Virginia Snyder make claims, only to have her deny that when offered the opportunity to present it or to present totally unprofessional results.

I believe that your newspaper should take the responsibility of going through the many and varied cases that she has made claim to and have been proven to he untrue and unworthy of belief in this county over the past decade.

I was not going to let him get away with that, so I wrote another letter to the editor of the *Boca Raton News*, which was published on the October 3 Editorial Page. I wrote in part:

If these charges were true, why didn't Bludworth prosecute me? I could have been charged with perjury and who knows how many other crimes....

Bludworth avoided answering the central question in my letter: "Why hasn't Bludworth told the public

the results of his probe into my theory of who killed
Richard Kreusler?"

Instead he viciously and irresponsibly attacked
me!

I challenge Bludworth to prove any of the statements
he made about my integrity, professionalism, ethics
or competency.

Bludworth never responded to my challenge and never made the
report public. However, that did not keep him from bad-mouthing me,
as I learned from reliable sources. He affected my business, because
many lawyers had become afraid to hire me to help their clients. He
was probably hoping to drive me out of business altogether. I persevered,
nevertheless.

Several years later, Jim Edwards—news editor for WJNO Radio
in West Palm Beach, who was very interested in Mark's case from the
beginning and not afraid to challenge the powers that be—managed
to get the report by threatening legal action. He also read all the files. I
was not surprised to learn from him that the witnesses gave Weissman
the same information they had given me. Jim also found additional
information in the files, withheld at the time of trial, which would have
supported my theory. I was very grateful to Jim. In the meantime, Mark
Herman was still in jail.

Also, a young woman attorney, Sharon Stedman, took up the cause.
Like Jim, she had become interested in the case when she read the trial
transcript. Now, and for eleven more years, she fought to free Mark,
finally succeeding when Mark was granted clemency in 1992—after
fifteen years in jail! Unfortunately, Jake-the-Snake was never charged
with the murder of Richard Kreusler.

As for Bludworth, he retired on his own after years as the elected
state's attorney for Palm Beach County. At least he was never able to get
elected to any other office, although he certainly tried.

THE DIAZ CASE:
CONVICTION

Luis Diaz was like a small animal caught in a steel trap—bewildered, hurting, wondering how he got into the trap and whether he would ever get out of it. The four sections in this book entitled "The Diaz Case," tell his story.

Luis Diaz was arrested in Dade County in August of 1979, and charged with eight counts of sexual assault as the Bird Road Rapist. I met him five months later, when Roy Black, his attorney, asked me to work on the case. As I questioned Diaz in jail through a Spanish interpreter, he started to cry. Tears of frustration ran down his cheeks as he protested his innocence. He had never harmed anybody, let alone raped any women.

Many criminals cry after they are arrested, some out of remorse, some in anger at being caught, some as an act. My instincts told me that the tears shed by Diaz were those of an innocent man. His responses were those of someone totally confused about what was happening and helpless to do anything about it.

Luis, his wife, and oldest son came to the United States from Cuba in 1967, when Luis was around thirty years old. They had two more children before they settled in Miami, where Luis worked the night shift as a fry cook in a Cuban restaurant. During the day, he made extra money by doing lawn work. He never learned English, so he usually took his oldest son with him to translate English to Spanish when he was soliciting work. The family had a modest house, which Luis had fixed up, near Bird Road, in south Miami.

In the previous two years, thirty-six sexual assaults had been committed in the area of the busy Bird Road between midnight and

5 a.m. A man would drive behind a female motorist and flick his headlights. Today, the average woman would know better than to stop. However, people were more trusting in the late 1970s.

These women thought that maybe there was something wrong with their car or that the other driver was someone they knew. When they pulled over and stopped, the rapist would force them into his car at gunpoint. Then he would drive somewhere, compelling the women to perform oral sex. When he reached his destination, he would rape them. Before releasing them, he took an item, such as their underwear or driver's license. Understandably, the surrounding communities were terrified and demanded that the police solve these crimes.

Luis's troubles started when a radio reporter who had been one of the rape victims accused him of the crime. She saw Luis by his car one morning and claimed that she recognized him as the man who raped her. However, she could not identify him in the subsequent police lineup and was very hesitant about picking him out of photos the police showed her later. Nevertheless, the police did not release him. Unfortunately for Luis, this was the second accusation against him.

He had been briefly questioned for the supposed rape of a teenage victim eighteen months earlier. That seventeen-year-old was working the register of a gas station one morning when Luis came in to get gas for his lawn mower. She was certain that he had the same car as the man who had raped her. Later, the police tracked the car to Luis. Luckily, he was released shortly, for he did not fit the description of the teenager's attacker as being six feet and weighing two hundred pounds. Luis is five feet, three inches and weighed 135 pounds. Another factor in his release was that the victim said her attacker spoke English, which Luis did not.

"You see," he told his wife at the time, "in this country, you have nothing to fear if you are innocent." That belief was soon to be shattered.

The Bird Road rapes continued the next year and a half, so when a second victim singled out Luis, the police thought that they had their man.

As soon as I became involved in the case, I decided to acquaint myself with the Diaz family. I knew that Luis finished work at Lila's Restaurant every night at eleven p.m. and that Caridad, his wife, picked him up and drove him home. If he had been slipping out of the house after midnight, night after night for two years, certainly his wife would have suspected something!

The Diaz house was neat and well kept. I noticed immediately that the car was parked on the driveway because the garage was used as a playroom for the children. This would become important information. Caridad and the three children welcomed me as I arrived. She offered me a cup of *café con leche* and shooed the two younger children out of the room. She explained that only fourteen-year-old Jose knew about their father's arrest. The other children thought their father was in the hospital.

Caridad proudly showed me the repairs and improvements that her husband had made to the house. At my request, she gave me a tour of the rooms, including the bedrooms. Caridad and Luis slept in a double bed, their room being just down the hall from the children's bedrooms. She stated emphatically that her husband was home every night. Indeed, I found it hard to believe that he was able to slip out of bed, get dressed or gather up his clothes to get dressed elsewhere, and go past the children's rooms and out to the car without waking anyone up.

Furthermore, even if he had managed to slip out to the car, the next-door neighbors would have heard him leaving and returning. As I had already noticed, Luis and Caridad always parked their car on the driveway. It was only ten paces from the neighbors' bedroom window. When I subsequently spoke with the neighbors, they said they never heard the Diaz car leave or return after Luis arrived home from work or before he left for work the next day.

In additional statements, Caridad told me that Luis did not own a gun and that he did not speak English. She explained that when they first came to the United States, they had lived in New Jersey, where many of the earlier Cuban immigrants resided. Luis signed up for English classes but dropped out after a week because of the long hours he worked. Since Caridad spoke English and the people Luis worked with were Cuban, he did not need to speak English in either New Jersey or, later, in Miami, after they moved.

She also told me that she would pick Luis up from work every night at eleven thirty. They would come home, and Luis would take a shower. His co-workers all said that he smelled of grease and onions when he finished. Then they would eat ice cream and watch television for a while before going to bed. Caridad said that there was no way he could leave the house and come back without her knowing it. She fiercely defended her husband, because she knew that he had done no wrong.

Jose, his oldest son, also firmly believed that his father was innocent. When Luis had been arrested in the middle of the night, he told his oldest son that now he was to be the head of the household and that he should look after his mother and the two younger children. It was obvious from Jose's solemn demeanor that he was taking his job very seriously. It was also very obvious that his heart was breaking and that he was near tears.

"When they came to arrest my father, they told me that he was the Bird Road Rapist, but I knew they were lying," he said. Later, Jose had a serious nervous breakdown.

It was becoming clear to me that Luis and his family were just as much victims of the Bird Road Rapist as the women who had been assaulted. It is interesting to note that after the trial, Channel 4 in Jacksonville hired a bilingual polygrapher who spent considerable time with Luis and who also became convinced of his innocence.

By the time Luis went to trial, I was certain that based on my own investigation, more than one man had committed the assaults, possibly three to five men who were associated with one another. This was the most reasonable conclusion I could draw, because the victims gave widely varying descriptions of their assailants and of the cars they drove. All said the man spoke English, but some said with a heavy Latin accent, others said with a light Latin accent. One woman who was Cuban said that her attacker was Anglo.

I know that height and weight are sometimes difficult for a victim of a violent crime to estimate, but not to such an extreme that they would describe their attacker as being over two hundred pounds and then pointing out Luis as the villain when he was only 135 pounds! Other specifics of their descriptions, such as gray hair, pockmarked face, and mustache should also have eliminated Luis as the rapist. He had a smooth complexion, no gray hair, and had never worn a mustache.

I believe I know why this tragedy happened. At one point before the trial, investigators had all the victims in a room together, discussing the attacks. I am certain that this event tainted each one's testimony or version of the events. In fact, they collaborated!

The fact that thorough police searches of Luis's car and residence turned up neither a gun nor any of the souvenirs the rapist had taken from his victims did not even cast enough doubt in the jurors' minds to prevent them from convicting Luis. I do not understand how this could have happened.

Why this travesty of justice? Community hysteria and the pressure on the police to quickly solve the crime played an important part. An even more disturbing and definitely related possibility is this: I believe the police framed Luis to get a quick conviction. Unfortunately, this was not the first time that police have railroaded a guilty verdict, nor am I naïve enough to believe it will be the last.

The evidence speaks for itself. To begin, at least two police officers wrote in their reports and testified at trial that they spoke to Luis in English. However, there were no tapes or notes of these interviews as proof of these conversations with Luis. These officers lied so that Luis would fit the victims' assertion that their attacker spoke English. In fact, Luis's co-workers at the restaurant swore that he did not even understand English and that they played jokes on him because of this.

Fred Mendez, a bilingual officer who testified, was another "official" witness who, in my opinion, destroyed the integrity of the trial. He actually fabricated statements about what witnesses told him. After the trial, the witnesses Mendez had interviewed told me that they had not made the statements attributed to them. Many of them said that they just shook their heads no and never spoke at all when asked if they knew anything.

Strangely, another officer who accompanied Mendez during these interviews but who did not speak Spanish left the police force right before the trial and moved to North Carolina. Certainly, this second officer knew that these witnesses did not give the lengthy statements Mendez had fabricated. No wonder he left the force and moved out of town for the trial. Even more interesting is that he returned to the force after the trial.

Mendez got away with lying on the witness stand. However, two years after the trial, he was charged with five counts of falsifying reports in five other cases. For twenty-six years I tried to use this information, plus other new evidence, to get Luis a new trial—to no avail. To make matters worse, Mendez received only a-slap-on-the-hand kind of censure for his actions and is still on the police force, as far as I know.

Luis's trial, which began May 5, 1980, lasted five days. Despite the questions about the state's evidence, especially the inconsistencies of the victims' descriptions of their attackers, the jury deliberated only three hours before convicting Luis Diaz of four rapes, three attempted rapes, five kidnappings, five robberies, and seven firearm charges. He was acquitted of one attempted rape. The judge gave him thirteen life sentences for the rapes, plus fifty-five years for the other counts. Luis would not be eligible for parole until 2006.

During the next few years, other lawyers worked on appeals for Luis, all of which were denied.

THE WILLIE
SIMPSON CASE

Our office often got death row cases from Palm Beach County years after the defendants' trials. Yet David Bludworth had been unhappy with me since the 1973 shooting of sixteen-year-old Eddie Cabrera, which was detailed earlier in this book. The police officer involved in the shooting claimed it was an accident, but evidence and witnesses pointed to a deliberate killing. Bludworth announced that he was personally going to investigate the shooting and then cleared the police officer. Eddie's father sued, and the city settled out of court for one hundred thousand dollars.

In 1983, Bludworth's office intimidated witnesses and lawyers who were working with me to get one of my clients off death row. One of their scare tactics involved the use of Florida's perjury law. As most people know, someone can be charged with perjury, which carries a five-year sentence for each count, if he or she is found to have lied under oath. What most people do not understand is that someone can also be charged with perjury if he or she gives conflicting statements under oath. The crime is not committed until the witness tells the second, conflicting story. This penalizes people who want to tell the truth at a second trial if they lied at the first.

The case in point concerns Willie Simpson, who was on death row for murdering a Delray police officer, John Kennedy. Simpson was innocent, but he had been convicted as a result of the false testimonies of two other criminals, Tony Hostzclaw and Melton Hunt. They had been offered the deal of less time for their crime if they would help the state put Willie away. After my thorough investigation of this case, I was convinced that John Kennedy had been murdered by drug dealers who were in cahoots with some of the police officers in the department. Kennedy had asked too many questions and written too many notes about what was happening in the department.

Obviously, these dirty cops did not want the real murderer caught, because they would be arrested for taking bribes from the drug lords. In looking for a suspect, they happened upon Willie, who was near the scene of the murder and had been in trouble before.

But now, one of the two witnesses who had lied at the first trial, Tony Hostzclaw, had had a change of heart. He wanted to tell the truth, because he was conscience-stricken.

When he confided in his minister, Semmie Taylor, Semmie suggested that Hostzclaw contact me, which he did. The other witness, Melton Hunt, also agreed to recant his former testimony and tell the truth, but only if I could guarantee him immunity from perjury when he changed his first story. This was something only Bludworth, as the state prosecutor, could do. Not only did Bludworth ignore my request for such immunity, which intimidated Hunt, he held Hostzclaw in jail and threatened him with perjury charges unless he went back to his original story.

To add more pressure, jail officials cut off all Willie's communication with me and prohibited his receiving any visitors. Hortzsclaw finally agreed not to change his original story. Willie Simpson, an innocent man, was on death row because two crooks had lied in order to get reduced sentences for their own crime. Bludworth was either covering up for corrupt police officers or denying that he was wrong the first time around—either way, this was a tragic example of how professional cronyism subverts the truth in our justice system.

Willie eventually got a new trial, and Hostzclaw testified he had originally lied about Willie's killing Kennedy. Unfortunately, Hunt stuck to his original story, and the defense attorney, Don Dowling, refused to call me as a witness to impeach Hunt's testimony. I found out after the trial that the prosecutor had warned Dowling that he would call a very credible witness, another lawyer, who would testify that I had falsified reports in another case to attack my credibility.

That same year, Bludworth's office tried to intimidate three other defense attorneys who were working on cases with me by threatening to destroy me on the witness stand if I were called to impeach any witness for the state. I suppose Bludworth thought that his scare tactic had worked so well with Dowling that he would try it again. Neither of the other attorneys paid any attention to him. In fact, one of them sent me a copy of Bludworth's letter containing the threat and urged me to sue him!

I did not sue. A lawsuit against a state's attorney would have totally disrupted my life, and it was only "he said, she said." I chose to represent the individuals who were the victims of injustice and in danger of losing their lives or freedom. At the same time, I was thwarting Bludworth and others like him every chance I got.

Hostzclaw's testimony was not enough to clear Willie of Kennedy's murder. He was now convicted of second-degree murder, but he was saved from the electric chair. I had to be satisfied with saving Willie's life, even though, at this writing, he is still in jail for a crime he did not commit. Bludworth has since retired.

ABUSE OF FEMALE PRISONERS IN PALM BEACH COUNTY

My first good look at conditions and abuses suffered by female prisoners in Palm Beach County jails came through the eyes of my clients who experienced them. I want to detail Judy Haas McNelis's story as an example of what goes on behind locked doors, both literally and figuratively.

When I first met Judy, in March of 1986, she was awaiting trial for first-degree murder. The forty-year-old mother of three had been convicted the year before of operating a large drug-smuggling business that brought marijuana to the United States from Jamaica. Two years earlier, shortly after her 1983 indictment on these charges, she had escaped from jail in Valdosta, Georgia, and was not caught until 1985, in Fort Lauderdale. Now, in addition to her twenty-year sentence for drug trafficking, Judy faced the death penalty for allegedly killing a pilot she had once hired.

Judy and the other female inmates had been transferred from the Palm Beach County Jail in downtown West Palm Beach to the Stockade, miles west of town, where only men were held previously. Officials said the second facility would be better for the women. If anything, it was worse, as I learned from working with Judy during the following year. At least the women in the old jail had access to hot water for coffee, tea, and instant soups!

Judy provided me with details of the abuses she and the other women suffered and of the bad conditions at the Stockade. Among her concerns was that women were denied local phone calls unless they called collect, even to their attorneys. Also, visiting hours were only two hours on Thursday mornings, instead of on weekends, as they were for men. Therefore, the women had difficulty communicating with the outside world and, in particular, with their families.

Furthermore, two-thirds of the inmates had not been convicted of any crime, but because they could not make bond, they had to await their trials in jail. Many had not even seen an attorney and did not know what they had been charged with.

Judy also gave my name to other women, who would call or write to me, begging for help. I was amazed at the compassion Judy felt for the other women in the Stockade while she awaited trial. It was as if her concern about being sentenced to the electric chair took second place to her concern for her cellmates.

In the meantime, the inmates suffered. Some of the problems one would expect—such as overcrowding, lack of air conditioning, and inadequate nutrition. However, the mistreatment or lack of treatment of the inmates could be life threatening. Judy told me about two pregnant girls who did not get vitamins or enough food to eat. Another woman, who was about five months pregnant when she arrived, lost ten pounds in the jail. She had begged for extra milk but got none. These women received no prenatal care.

Judy also told me about Gertrude, who had a bad wound to her foot from a car accident that occurred before she was brought in. The nurse just gave her a bottle of hydrogen peroxide to pour over the wound and left. No one ever came to the cell to bandage the foot. Gertrude was middle-aged and obese and could not tend to her foot without great difficulty. To make matters worse, she did not even get to see a doctor for another two weeks. Luckily for her, Judy cleaned and bandaged the foot each day to prevent infection.

Indeed, there were numerous complaints about the callousness of the medical staff. A woman suffered from a toothache and swollen jaw for weeks before she got to see a dentist. Another inmate, Billie Jo, was in agony for days because a nerve was exposed from a partial root canal. When I called the medical staff to complain, some of the officials at the Stockade told Billie Jo never to call Virginia Snyder for anything. However, many of the women continued to call me, because they learned from Judy that I would accept their collect calls and that I would write letters and make phone calls on their behalf.

For instance, almost all of the inmates had head lice. Although they were given medication for their hair, nothing was done to sterilize the bed linens, so they were constantly re-infected. I called the Health Department, and then bed linens were cleaned. Unfortunately, the mattresses and pillows were not disinfected, so the problem went on. I continued to complain. Other acts of callousness occurred every day: when one of Judy's cellmates had a grand mal seizure, the nurse did not come for thirty minutes after she had been called. In another case, a prisoner was having dizzy spells, fainting, and blacking out. She had to wait two weeks to get medication after she saw the doctor.

Other times, the mistreatment was degrading. For example, the women often had to go without toilet paper for hours at a time, several times a week, until a friendly guard answered their request. In the meantime, if they had to go to the toilet, they used their washcloths and washed them out as thoroughly as they could. That is, if the guards had not stolen their soap, which they did about twice a month when they came into the cells to check for contraband.

According to the rules, women were not allowed to go to the toilet until their meal trays were picked up. One girl had to use the facilities and could not wait, so the guard took the TV away as a punishment. Fortunately, a nicer guard on a different shift gave it back. Women were also humiliated when they asked for sanitary napkins and had to wait for as many as five hours before a guard brought them. As a result, inmates often had blood on their uniforms and had to wash the stains out later. They had nothing else to wear while they did this.

On August 3, 1986, I compiled a list of these complaints and circulated them to a number of agencies and individuals. I called Mildred "Mim" George, director of social services and alternative sentencing for the Public Defender's Office, for help. She sent people from her office or went herself to counsel the inmates. Other caring friends, such as Adele Kaserman, coordinator for the County's Commission on the Status of Women; Alice Coane, past president of the National Organization for Women; and Harriet Glasner, president of the American Civil Liberties Union in Florida, joined my crusade to change the deplorable conditions of the Stockade. We mostly used the skunk approach, making the biggest stink we could until conditions gradually improved over the next two years.

After numerous written reports to and testimony before various state committees concerned with the bad conditions for women at the Stockade, we were successful in 1988, when the Florida State Legislature passed the Parity in Programs statute. Now female inmates would be treated with more dignity and have the same rights as male inmates. These rights included the use of a law library and participation in work-release programs. In the late 1990s, a new and much improved wing was built at the Stockade. All of the correctional officers are female.

After her last visit to the Stockade, Mim George said, "It was difficult to believe that this was the same place where all the terrible things took place a few years ago." This case is another example of how a small group of people can fight city hall and succeed.

None of this would have been possible without Judy, who kept us informed of all the specifics. However, we also had our own Deep Throat at the time, a correctional officer who confirmed everything that Judy and the other inmates were telling us. She was deeply concerned about the horrible mistreatment of the inmates and was in constant contact with Mim. To this day, I do not know her name, but I do know that she went back to school and got a degree in mental health counseling, which she now does professionally.

All the time we were trying to improve conditions at the Stockade, I was working on Judy's case, which was set for trial. As stated earlier, she was accused of having her pilot, Frank Marrs, killed by the two men who would now testify against her.

The 1980 unsolved murder had finally been "solved" after Judy's escape. Two other men who worked for her in the drug-smuggling business, John Parella and Gary Childers, had pled guilty to killing the pilot. At the same time, they fingered Judy as one of two people who had ordered the hit. In exchange for their cooperation, they received sentences of fifteen years for second-degree murder.

"It was necessary for the state to make plea agreements with these men to get to the masterminds," Assistant State Attorney Georgia Boome said. The other "mastermind" whom they testified against, Jean Tumulty, had already been tried and convicted of the pilot's murder.

Parella and Childers could have faced the death penalty had they gone to trial. Judy, who had been on the run at the time of these events, was facing her own trial now. She told me that she was innocent of the murder, and I believed her.

When I took the case, I learned that Parella, one of the convicted men who would testify for the prosecution, had a record of kidnapping and attempted murder. The victim of that attempted murder was Robert Bazzano, who had also been involved in drug trafficking. Our office tracked him down after we learned that one year before the pilot's murder, Buzzano was also supposed to be murdered. He was lured to an isolated spot, shot five times, robbed of fifty thousand dollars, and left for dead.

The assailant was John Parella. The victim was permanently paralyzed, but he lived. I believed that there were too many parallels between what happened to Bazzano and what happened to Frank Marrs to be coincidental. After we found Bazzano, he agreed to testify for the defense. Diane Craig, who interned with me and who then worked with us as an investigator, deserves the credit for finding Buzzano and convincing him to testify. It was no easy job.

Judy's trial began February 2, 1987. Parella and Childers, the other witness against Judy, testified that Judy ordered them to kill Marrs because she did not want to pay the pilot for the last load of marijuana he flew in. As a result, Marrs was threatening to hold the plane. Judy testified that she met with Marrs the night before his murder and had dinner with him. At that time, she paid him twenty thousand dollars toward the money she owed him. The money was never found. Judy's attorney argued that Parella killed Marrs for the twenty thousand, just as he had tried to kill Bazzano for the fifty thousand a year earlier.

The highlight of the trial was Bazzano's testimony. Seated in his wheelchair, he calmly recounted the events of his near killing. Parella had gotten out of his car to relieve his bladder. When Bazzano left the vehicle to do the same, Parella shot him five times.

"The third shot paralyzed me," he stated matter-of-factly.

In his confession to the police, Parella had said that the men got out of the car to urinate when he shot Marrs. The trial lasted seven days, but the jury took only three hours to find Judy not guilty. A week later, I received this wonderful letter from Judy:

My Dear Sweet Virginia,

No one will ever know and words are totally inadequate when trying to express the heartfelt thanks that I feel for you.

I had no one here, no family, no friends, in jail, and such a jail, accused of first-degree murder. You were my lifeline—not only mine but the only resource that all the poor women out here had. When we were sick—call Virginia. When we couldn't get information on cases, times, dates or even what some of us were accused of—call Virginia. When there were no silver linings but only dark clouds—you were the ray of hope that kept not only me going, but so many, many others.

When I say I wouldn't have made it without you, it is the literal truth. You are a friend of mine.

Love, Forever,
(signed)
Judy

The Diaz Case: Years of Frustration

Right after the trial in the Luis Diaz case, the judge needed to approve my bill for the time I spent on the case. During this hearing, he made an important statement.

Flipping through my records with his forefinger, the judge said, "I examined the entire file, which is very thick. I read it, the whole thing. Suddenly, after reading it, I am not as convinced as I was before about [Diaz's] guilt."

Not only did he approve my fee, he then appointed me to continue investigating the case. Unfortunately, the judge left the bench a short time later. This was a bad break, because I believe that he could have helped us. Nevertheless, I continued to work for twenty-six years without compensation to prove Luis's innocence.

I began to find new evidence, and each time I did, my hopes soared. Most importantly, I believe that I found out who the real Bird Road Rapist was. Actually, it was a small gang of three men. This new evidence emerged when Caridad visited her husband in prison a few months after the trial. Luis told her that he had just had a strange experience.

Another inmate, also a Cuban, said to him in private in Spanish, "I feel sympathy for you."

"Why?" Diaz asked.

"Because you're innocent," he replied as he walked away.

When Caridad repeated this information to me, I became very interested and told her to have her husband find out this inmate's name. I learned that he was Luis Nunez, so I went to the Dade County

Courthouse to look up his record, which was extensive. I noticed that he was involved with a small gang in a number of crimes and that Juan Delatorre, a well-known criminal, seemed to be the leader of the gang.

On one of my trips to the state prison to see another client (and also to see Luis, which I did whenever I was in the prison), I asked permission to visit Nunez. He stared at me with his cold, blue eyes when I introduced myself and asked him if he knew Juan Delatorre. He said nothing. Indeed, Nunez looked like a death's head with his sunken cheeks and shaved head. I then explained why I had come to see him and asked for his help in identifying the actual Bird Road Rapists. Still he said nothing. I waited a few more minutes.

Just as I was about to leave, he finally spoke, in English, "You're on the right track." He would not elaborate, however.

I left my card with him, saying, "Let me know if I can ever be of help to you."

I also wrote him on occasion to keep up the contact. I was surprised when he finally wrote back. He asked me if I could get his medical records for him, because he was not allowed to see them. He signed a release, and I was able to get the records he wanted. I felt certain that he would help with the Diaz case now and looked forward to our next conversation. My hopes were up, only to be dashed by the news that Nunez had escaped from the prison before I could speak to him again.

I kept track of his case, hoping that he would soon be captured, but I had to wait five years. During those years I often communicated with Diaz, who would send cards with a message in Spanish. Underneath would be an English translation by another inmate. When I saw Luis in prison, we hugged, and he cried, all the while thanking me for continuing to help him. I promised that I would never stop until he was free. Another of my clients interpreted for us and told me that inmates and guards alike believed Luis to be an innocent victim of the criminal justice system. A prison chaplain who had come to know Luis contacted me, offering to do anything to help him. Luis spent most of his time in prison reading the Bible.

In 1983, during the five years that Nunez was "on the lam," I got some good news. Donna Coppage, one of the women who had originally identified Diaz as the Bird Road Rapist, had recanted. She said that the man who had to be her attacker had recently followed her. Now Ms. Coppage realized that she had identified the wrong man at the trial and wanted to right the wrong. She explained that she had not recognized her attacker in any of the pictures the police showed her in the first photo lineup. The police insisted that she keep looking at these same photos, even though she asked to see other pictures.

She finally selected Diaz, because he was the only one who remotely resembled her rapist.

I took her statement to Janet Reno, then district attorney for Dade County, who was the original prosecuting attorney. After much insistence on my part, she assigned an assistant district attorney to review the case. This assistant attorney conducted his review by merely rereading all of the original testimony and concluded that Diaz was guilty. He had never even interviewed Donna Coppage!

I kept calling Reno, insisting that someone interview Coppage and those other witnesses who had never been called to testify at the first trial. I told her that Fred Mendez's testimony needed to be reviewed in light of the charges brought against him after the trial. I kept sending her "to-do" lists to make it easier for her office to investigate. Finally, Reno agreed to take another look at the case and assigned her chief investigator to do the job. He took months and months before he finished reading the one thousand pages of court testimony and concluded that Diaz was guilty. Again, he had not interviewed Coppage, the victim who was trying to help me free Luis Diaz.

My ability to remain emotionally detached failed me in this case. As a former investigative reporter and now a private investigator, I knew that I had to turn off my emotions when working and use my "back burner" during intervals. However, I was haunted by my sympathy for Luis because of the great injustice done to him, by my anger at those responsible, and by my frustration at not getting anyone in authority to help us.

Finally, we got a break. Luis Nunez, who had escaped five years earlier, was captured and back in prison. I was desperate for his help and could not wait to interview him again. Indeed, I believed that Nunez was the answer to Luis's problems, and he gave me more and more information every time I visited him. He told me I was right about Juan Delatorre being the gang leader and then gave me the names of the three members of the gang who were collectively the Bird Road Rapist.

Nunez insisted that he did not take part in any of the rapes because he had two young daughters. He also told me where they got the cars to commit their crimes. In addition, he explained that he and the rest of the gang were heavily involved in drug trafficking across the country, in the course of which they paid off the police. Most importantly, he signed a sworn affidavit. Ten years had passed since Luis had been sent to prison. Now I would get Janet Reno to reopen the case.

THE RUTH ANN NEDERMIER MURDER CASE

Ruth Ann Nedermier was a seventy-two year-old retired schoolteacher, who taught at Belvedere Elementary School in West Palm Beach for over twenty years. She was murdered and her body dismembered at the beginning of March in 1988. The decomposing parts of her body were found in a steamer trunk, which was four feet long, two feet wide, and three feet deep, less than a mile from my office in Delray Beach. Although I specialized in murder cases, this one shocked me, not only because of the heinous nature of the crime, but also because the victim was close to my own age, sixty-six.

We were hired by the defense attorney to investigate the case. Shortly thereafter, I remember looking out of my office window at the butterfly garden I had planted and at the flowering trees I loved. I had always felt safe here. Ruth Nedermier had lived alone in a little house surrounded by a garden in a quiet neighborhood like mine. She had probably felt safe there also.

Suspicion soon focused on Inger Lemont, a twenty-three-old health care employee who had worked for the victim the previous six months. Lemont, a Boca Raton High School graduate and former U.S. Army reservist, had stolen seventeen thousand dollars from Nedermier's bank account. Now Lemont was missing from her Lake Worth apartment. (The bank had become aware of the forged checks a few days before Ruth Ann disappeared, and they stated that they had talked to someone at her house. I later found out that Inger had intercepted this phone call.) We were familiar with many cases of health care workers robbing their elderly patients, but this was the first time we had known a health care worker murdering the victim.

Ruth Ann was first reported missing on March 4, when her physical therapist found no one home for a regularly scheduled session. There was no sign of burglary, and it was evident to the investigators that Ruth Ann had not left for an errand or a visit, because she was recovering from hip surgery and still used a walker. Thirteen days later, Inger's father found the body parts in a trunk in his closet when he investigated a foul odor. He immediately notified the police, who were already looking for Inger and two or three men seen in a car at Nedermeier's house the afternoon she was reported missing.

The police identified the body by a serial number found on the hip implant.

When Inger had her brother bring the trunk to her parents' home, she told her mother it contained things for church. She told her sister it contained stolen meat. She had told her father nothing. When she turned herself in on March 17, she told the police the meat story also. She said that some men claiming to be salesmen came to her apartment trying to sell meat and then left the trunk on her patio.

More evidence implicating Inger in the murder was found about six blocks from the Lemont home. A teenager looking for candy in a trash bin behind the local McCroy store found Nedermier's credit cards, personal papers, house keys, and shattered eyeglasses. He also found a bloodstained brick, a small, bloodstained towel, and a prescription vial with Ruth Ann's name on it. When police searched the Lemont house, they found bloodstained clothing belonging to Inger.

Although I believed that Inger was definitely involved in the murder, I could not believe that she, just an average-sized woman, had moved Ruth Ann's body from West Palm Beach to her apartment in Lake Worth and then dismembered the body by herself. Not surprisingly, police were looking for Inger's live-in boyfriend, Gregory O. Howard. He was a former Palm Beach County Sheriff's deputy who had been forced to resign for allegedly trying to force sex on a female deputy.

During my investigation, I tried to get Inger to tell me if her boyfriend was involved. She denied that he had anything to do with the murder or dismemberment. She also denied that she did.

However, I found more damaging evidence against her when I learned that she was arrested in 1986 and pleaded guilty to stealing eight thousand dollars worth of jewelry from an elderly Delray Beach woman for whom she worked. In a letter she had written to the judge, Inger said that she was very remorseful for the crime and felt that further incarceration would hinder her career. She begged for forgiveness. As a result, she received only a ninety-day sentence, although she was forced to pay $3,300 restitution. Inger was released from jail on March 28, 1987, and placed on probation.

Given Inger's criminal history, I was puzzled as to how she could have worked as a home health aide. It turned out that a nursing service sent Inger to Ruth Ann before checking her credentials. After a week, the personnel director said they no longer used Inger because of what they described as "unreliability." It is not clear if they ever learned about her criminal history. Unfortunately, Nedermier then hired Inger independently.

Finally, on March 19, in a conversation with the police, Inger implicated her boyfriend in the murder. She said that he had repeatedly told her that they "should rob the old bitch." In her deposition, she said, "But I did not know Greg was going to hit her in the head with a brick."

In the one-hundred-page statement, Inger said that she gave the money she stole to her boyfriend to buy drugs. Right after the bank called about the forged checks, she called Howard. He and an accomplice looked through Ruth Ann's bedroom for jewels and money while Inger distracted the victim elsewhere. However, Ruth Ann saw the men and began hobbling back to her bedroom with her aluminum walker. That was when Howard struck her with the brick. Howard then dragged her body out of the house with his accomplice and took it to Inger's apartment in Lake Worth. At the same time, Inger took her three-year-old son to her parents in Delray Beach for the weekend.

Sunday morning, she gave her boyfriend money to buy a chainsaw, gloves, and three packages of large garbage bags. She stayed in the living room while Howard dismembered the body and wrapped the parts in the garbage bags, "the biggest ones you could buy," so they would fit into the trunk that she had bought a week earlier for two hundred dollars. Then they filled the rest of the trunk with mothballs. Howard was going to take the trunk and burn it. Instead, he disappeared.

The trunk stayed in Inger's apartment until the following Thursday, when she got her brother to help her take it to her parents' home. She threw Ruth Ann's purse into a dumpster in Delray Beach and the chainsaw into a dumpster in Boynton Beach.

Inger appeared to be completely remorseless and unfeeling as she told her story (even though she had tried to kill herself in the Palm Beach County Jail after she was arrested). I believed her story.

Nevertheless, Howard was never charged with the crime. The police never even tried to find out about the men in the car who were seen outside Ruth Ann's house the same afternoon she was reported missing. Howard turned state's evidence against his former girlfriend. On June 7, 1989, Inger pleaded guilty to second-degree murder. The state attorney said she would probably be behind bars for twenty years. Her attorney said that Inger accepted the plea, knowing the alternative could have been the death penalty.

There is no doubt in my mind that Inger's boyfriend, Gregory O. Howard, should have been charged also, and no doubt that this was another case of a prosecutor giving a deal to one of the perpetrators in order to get a quick conviction of the other. It is obvious why Howard would get the deal instead of Inger: he was less vulnerable than she because he had been a Palm Beach County Sheriff's deputy and knew how to protect himself. That he got away with such a grisly crime still upsets me.

Of the eighty-eight murders in Palm Beach County in 1988, this was by far the most cold-blooded. That the victim was an elderly invalid made it even more heinous. Connie Chung of ABC's *20/20* thought so and featured it on her program titled "Aging" on July 12, 1988.

JIMMY SHEPHERD

The body of sixteen-year-old Jimmy Shepherd, the youngest of sixteen children, was found in June of 1982, in Delray Beach, near the Linton Bridge along the Intracoastal Waterway. His death was attributed to a cocaine overdose, but my investigations showed that he was murdered.

Omar Galvez is a Marielito, one of the Cubans released from prisons or mental hospitals by Fidel Castro and put on boats to Miami in 1980. He is a pedophile who has molested, threatened, and terrorized teenage boys and their families. I came to know of him in January of 1988. Don Ralph, of Ralph's Buick, hired me to stop Galvez from terrorizing his teenage son and the family. In the course of my investigation, I spoke to many youths and their parents who had encountered Galvez, and I subsequently got numerous charges brought against him, most of which were eventually dropped because of his involvement with the police. At the same time, I realized that Galvez was responsible for the murder of Jimmy Shepherd six years earlier.

Galvez desired blond, junior high school boys, whom he lured into his car ostensibly for drugs and alcohol, but literally for sex. The state of Jimmy Shepherd's corpse was indicative of how Galvez worked. The dead boy was found with his pants down and (although maggots were already eating his body) with his penis erect. I still cringe whenever I think of the hideous police photos. There was evidence that his wrists had been tied. More disturbing, I learned that semen was found on anal swabs of the victim's rectum but that this evidence had never been sent to the FBI by the Delray Police Department. Somehow, it was lost.

This evidence was crucial to the case, because Galvez and other pedophiles put cocaine up their victims' rectums to enhance their erections and thus the ensuing sex. I believe that Galvez used too much cocaine on Jimmy and that the youth died during the sexual encounter. His erect penis after death and the coroner's findings of a cocaine overdose as the cause of death led me to my conclusion. Also, there was never any evidence to show that Jimmy used cocaine. Apparently, when Galvez realized what had happened, he dumped the body and fled.

Before he had sex with his victims, according to the numerous youths I interviewed while working for the Ralph family, Galvez plied them with drugs and alcohol, all the while secretly recording his conversations with them with a cassette recorder he hid under his car seat. If the boys then refused his sexual advances, Galvez threatened to expose their indiscretions by playing the tape for their parents and teachers. I believe that this is what happened to Jimmy. I even found a witness who saw Jimmy get into Galvez's car after he put his bicycle in the trunk on the day of his death.

I wrote and sent a lengthy report to the city commission about what I perceived as brutality in the Delray Police Department at the time, including the Shepherd case. The commissioners then forwarded the letter to the governor's office. Governor Bob Martinez appointed Janet Reno as special prosecutor to investigate the allegations in my report. She chose Florida Department of Law Enforcement Agent (FDLE) Don Ugliano to review Jimmy's death. Ugliano was dismayed that important evidence was missing; however, even after combing through what evidence there was, he was convinced that Galvez had murdered Jimmy.

Upon reading Ugliano's findings, Reno decided that indeed there was enough evidence to get an indictment from the grand jury. However, she was not certain there was enough evidence to convict. So she dropped the whole matter.

I disagreed with her decision; if the prosecutor could get an indictment, the state should have let a jury decide whether to convict after hearing all of the evidence. What a disappointment! After all these years, I have not forgotten about Jimmy. In fact, I contacted Ugliano in 2005, and we decided that he should look for DNA evidence to reopen the case. Sadly, he reported back that all evidence in the case has been lost. I have not given up.

I worked hard to get Galvez off the streets. In 1988, Galvez was charged with aggravated assault and lewd assault on Don Ralph's son. Unfortunately, he was found not guilty of trying to hire men to break the legs and arms of Ralph's son, and he was released on bond on December 28, 1989. Galvez has managed to evade almost all of the charges brought against him by the boys and their families. His "Teflon" status was assured when Galvez became an informant for more of the local, state, and federal law enforcement agencies in South Florida.

Finally, I was able to alert the Delray Beach community to what Galvez was doing by getting Fox Broadcasting to do a story about him for its program *The Reporter*. The network sent a crew down to Delray Beach to interview victims, witnesses, parents, police officers, and me. The episode was titled "Omar, the Evil." The resulting publicity enraged the police department and Galvez. He decided to come after me.

On Sunday afternoon, May 13, 1990, Galvez cut off my car as I was driving north on Federal Highway in Boynton Beach. He jumped out of his vehicle and came running toward me, all the while threatening to kill me and to throw my body into a canal. I realized that he was holding a mini cassette recorder, pointing it as if it were a gun. He was hoping that I would threaten him so that he would have this on tape.

Instead, I shouted, "It's May 13, 1990, and Omar Galvez is threatening to kill me!"

His face contorted in anger, and he hit me in the jaw with the recorder. I saw the blow coming but did not have time to roll up the window. I did jerk my head back so that I suffered less injury. Two young men traveling in the opposite direction saw what was happening, crossed the median, and came to my aid. When Galvez saw them, he jumped into his car and fled.

I had mixed emotions. I was plenty scared but also happy. Galvez's attack on me would come under the recently enacted Crimes Against the Elderly law because I was over sixty-five; in fact, I was sixty-nine. After trying unsuccessfully to get the charge dropped or reduced, Galvez pleaded no contest and was found guilty of crimes against the elderly. I was elated, even though he was sentenced only to time served awaiting trial.

As late as 1994, Galvez was still working as a confidential informant and terrorizing young boys. The bad publicity, including "Omar, the Evil," caused him to leave Delray Beach and move to West Palm Beach, where I understand he prefers Hispanic teenage boys. Time-consuming attempts have been made by several politicians in the mid-nineties, namely then U.S. Congressman Dan Mica and then State Representative

Steve Press, to get Galvez deported, but to no avail. At least he should have been held indefinitely at the Krome [Federal] Detention Center in Dade County.

THE GERALD PALLER CASE

Professional cronyism is responsible for corrupt attorneys protecting their own, as it was in Mark Herman's case. Professional cronysim is responsible for police protecting their own, as it was in Willie Simpson's case. Professional cronyism is also responsible for policemen killing their own, as I believe it was in Captain Gerald "Jerry" Paller's case, which follows.

Paller's death, on November 17, 1988, was officially ruled a suicide, but the more information I picked up from friendly police officers, city employees who knew Paller, and anonymous callers, the more convinced I became that he was murdered.

To begin, there was no suicide note. Furthermore, Jerry had made plans with a friend the night before to meet for a bagel break the morning of his death. Jerry had also called another friend that same night to report that work was going well. Jerry was in charge of recruiting new police officers for the department, and he and his friend chatted for over half an hour.

Jerry's body was found propped up on a couch by the sliding back door. A neighbor told me that this door was never locked. His gun was lying on his chest. The bullet that went through Jerry's head and dropped down between the studs in the wall behind him was not recovered, so no one proved that it came from Jerry's gun. As far as I know, the spent casing was never found, nor was the holster.

Most disturbing, the crime scene was not secured. The couch on which the body was laying was carried out and taken away. No blood spatter expert was called in, and the blood spatter that was on the wall had been washed off. Finally, there was no neighborhood canvass done to learn if anyone living in the area had seen or heard anything that morning.

Paller was known as a straight shooter in the department, an officer who would not be a part of corruption or police brutality. In fact, I learned that Paller had a falling out with his boss, Chief Kilgore, about a ticket-fixing incident.

"Paller had put 'void per chief ' on a ticket fixed for a former city employee," a friend of Jerry told me. Then he added, "[Jerry] told me about three weeks before his death that when Janet Reno got there, he would probably be the only one left upstairs [in administration]."

It was commonly believed that Paller knew everything that was going on in the department, although as a good company man, he would never blow the whistle. However, I concluded, it is one thing to keep quiet on one's own and quite another to face questioning under oath by a special prosecutor called in to investigate the department.

I did not know him or his family and was hesitant to intrude on the family's grief. Unfortunately, they moved away before I had a chance to meet Jerry's wife, Darlene. When I was planning this book, in April of 2004, I decided to locate Darlene. I learned that she had remarried and that her name was now Rutland. The family was living in Vermont. After I made contact, she and her son David came to see me.

Darlene told me how traumatic Jerry's death had been for the whole family. She still felt torn by guilt because she had not recognized that he was suicidal. The children, David and Joanna, could not understand why their father had chosen to leave them.

"David never got over his father's death," she told me. "It affected his whole life.

"He was going to take me to a ball game that night," David said.

The tall, handsome pre-med student was very interested in my theory that his father had been murdered. I gave him my lengthy file and watched as the realization dawned on him that his father did not commit suicide and abandon them.

"I'm going to get to the bottom of this," David vowed after he read my notes. "Mrs. Snyder, will you work with me?'"

Darlene went through the same transition as her son while she listened to my information and read the files. She gladly filled in the missing links in my knowledge about the morning of her husband's death.

On the morning of November 17, 1988, Jerry had gotten up earlier than his wife. When the alarm went off, he came running back to the bedroom to flip it off, said, "Sorry, Babe," and went back to the family room to continue reading the newspaper.

While Darlene Paller was still in bed, she heard the shot, ran through the house, and found him on the couch with his gun lying on his chest.

"There was blood everywhere," she told me.

"Two weeks before his death, he called in sick. I remember sitting by his bedside and holding his hand. 'Are you sick or upset?' I asked him.

"'A little of both,' he replied.

"'Do you want to talk to someone?'

"'Who could I talk to?'"

Darlene continued. "I suggested Bill Cochrane, then the assistant chief, but Jerry refused. 'I can't,' he said."

Almost as an afterthought, Darlene mused, "I always wondered what happened at his meeting with Janet Reno."

"What?" I exclaimed in surprise.

"Yes, about two weeks before his death, Jerry dressed in his suit and said that he was going down to meet with Janet Reno. He was gone most of the day, and when he returned, he would not tell me what happened except to say, 'I'm on my own.'"

I believe that his murder had some connection to the upcoming investigation of the Delray Police Department by special prosecutor Janet Reno. This investigation was the result of my lengthy report to the city commissioner in 1988, as explained earlier in this book in "The Jimmy Shepherd Case." Several confidential sources had told me that Chief Charles Kilgore and the upper echelon were very worried that Reno's investigation would "blow everything wide open." In fact, Kilgore resigned shortly before Reno issued her report in May of 1991, even though her report concluded that there was insufficient evidence to bring criminal charges against the Delray Police Department.

"If Jerry had lived and been questioned by Janet, he would have put an end to everything," one officer told me.

Even though this was not a case of mine, it was a concern of mine. I was responsible for the appointment of Janet Reno to investigate the

Delray Police Department, and I wanted to see justice done for Captain Paller.

The day of Jerry's death, Paller's friend and neighbor overheard Police Chief Charles Kilgore saying, "That fucking Virginia Snyder and Janet Reno, how many more are they going to kill?" The friend quickly reported the statement to me.

At the funeral service, the reverend told mourners, "He couldn't compromise the truth, even if it caused him deep frustration and anguish."

Not long after, I received an anonymous call about the priest. "He knows a lot, but he is scared to death," the caller said.

I had already decided that the priest probably did know a lot, because Jerry was a Eucharistic minister in the same church. While confessions are sacrosanct, information and concerns shared with a priest are not. I knew that the priest was a close family friend, so I tried to make an appointment with him to discuss what he might know about Paller's death. However, after numerous phone calls that were never returned, I gave up trying to meet with him.

Nevertheless, while David was still in Florida, he decided to speak with this same priest, of whom he had fond memories. David was very disappointed with the reception he received from his father's former friend, however. The priest's refusal to remember anything or to be helpful supported the information I had been given by the anonymous caller, that the priest was scared to death.

The meeting David had with the current police chief, Larry Schroeder, was just as unsatisfying. This did not surprise me either, because I had been pressuring the chief for some time to reopen the Paller death case.

Also, David's attempts to find out about his father's meeting with Janet Reno were unsatisfying. There is no record of such a meeting. David even spoke to a secretary who had been in Janet Reno's office at the time, but she had no recollection of any meeting.

I still believe that Jerry went to Reno's office, but he may have spoken to someone else who worked for her. The question nagging at me after all these years is whether that trip was the cause of his death.

Certainly, the following conversation, which occurred May 18, 1992, lends credence to my theory. The exchange occurred between a city employee, who is a friend of mine, and an officer of the Delray

Police Department. They talked for several hours, during which time the officer expressed his frustration and anger about certain changes in Delray Beach.

"Since that damn Rodney King beating, the new chief won't let us do anything," he complained. "When Kilgore [who was forced to resign] was chief, he was a straight shooter; he stood behind his officers. He would allow the police to take care of the blacks when they would get out of hand. With this new chief, we can't do a thing."

He then proceeded to tell my friend about that "fat bitch, Virginia Snyder. It's all her fault, what happened to Kilgore. That woman's nothing but trouble. Her nose is in all the city business, screwing up the town. Stay away from her."

My friend did not enlighten the officer about our relationship.

Comparing the two chiefs, the officer said, "If a riot would start [in Delray Beach], I believe the new chief would tell me to go someplace and hide. You wouldn't believe some of the blacks they're hiring now. This new police aide they just pushed up, he can't even fill out a form. I see all kinds of shit going on in this city, but I can't discuss it."

My friend then asked a question. "What about all the crack houses?"

"I'll tell you something off the record. This city is run through dirty politics and corruption."

The officer continued at length about different policemen who got into trouble because they were caught with prostitutes and underage girls. He mentioned one sergeant who went with underage girls for years, and everybody knew it. "It was condoned," he said.

After more talk about the problems of individual men on the force, the officer brought up the subject of suicide. "You've heard about all these suicides?" He was referring to other suicides connected to the police department. Then he mentioned Paller.

My friend commented that he remembered hearing something to the effect that it was murder.

At that, the officer became very upset and snapped. "Why did you say that?"

Their conversation ended abruptly when the very talkative officer suddenly had nothing more to say.

VIRGINIA SNYDER VERSUS THE CITY AND POLICE DEPARTMENT OF DELRAY BEACH

My campaign to draw attention to the corruption in the Delray Police Department continued, despite the many disappointments I had in fighting against the system. I refused to give up, and I was not afraid of any consequences to me personally. In fact, this cause was a priority, so much so that the Delray Police Department wiretapped my office to get evidence of any kind to use against me and close up my business. They countered my campaign with their own; get rid of Virginia Snyder!

Everything came to a head in 1989. A young woman, whose first name was Nancy and whose father was a former city attorney, showed up at my office one day. She wanted me to take her on as an intern and train her to become a private investigator. I explained that I did not want an intern at that time but that she could come to the office as much as she liked, and I would teach her how to do research at the County Courthouse in West Palm Beach. I knew and respected her father, so I wanted to help Nancy get started.

She always showed up with a briefcase, which I assumed was an expression of her desire to be a private investigator. Nancy spent time in my office and then went to the courthouse to practice research. She was with me a few months. I did not have much hope for her success, because she seemed very flighty. I later learned that she was reportedly on drugs.

One afternoon, about three months after Nancy showed up at my office, I received a call from a clerk at the West Palm Beach County Courthouse. She said, "There's an envelope here filled with documents that have your letterhead on them. They've been sitting here since this morning, and I finally decided to open the envelope to determine whose it was. No one has come back to claim it."

I was puzzled and alarmed. Ross drove to the West Palm Beach County Courthouse to get the envelope. When I examined it, I noticed a small, handwritten note on one of the back corners. No question about it, the distinctive handwriting was Nancy's. When I called her, she refused to speak to me. I contacted her father, who was very upset to learn that Nancy had taken documents out of my office without permission.

I later learned that Nancy had been used by the Delray Police Department to secretly steal my documents so that certain members of the police department could copy them. Also, on at least two occasions, she carried a recording device in her briefcase so that Major Richard Lincoln, who was sitting in his car about one hundred feet from my office, could listen to my conversations.

In other words, the Delray Police Department had used her as a mole. According to their arrangement, if she would act as an informant, they would fix her numerous traffic tickets. In fact, they had used her as an informant before under the same circumstances. Fortunately, in one of her flighty moments, she had left documents at the courthouse.

However, she managed to steal over two hundred pages from my office files before that time. This was relatively easy to do because of the way my office was set up in our home. First of all, the upright file cabinets were located in plain sight behind my desk. If I went to the kitchen to make a cup of coffee or used the bathroom, Nancy had easy access to everything if Ross and Wayne, my partners, were also gone.

There were times when I looked for a document that was missing and muttered, "I thought I had that" or "Did I misfile that?"

When I realized what had been happening, I was furious! Secretly copying my documents and taping my conversations without getting warrants was illegal. I called every newspaper, television and radio station, and I held a news conference to expose this corruption. In addition, I filed a lawsuit against the city and four members of the police department of Delray Beach, including Chief Charles Kilgore. I insisted on a letter of apology, which was more important to me than any damages I might receive.

Ten years later, the letter arrived. By that time, the hierarchy at the city and police department had changed, and the new leaders, in the spirit of reconciliation, wanted to end the lawsuit. The new mayor, David W. Schmidt, wrote the letter, which I include at the end of this section.

I savored the victory of the lawsuit, but I am still frustrated and disappointed that the corruption I have fought against all these years has never been properly addressed. The individuals responsible have never been brought to justice. Yes, there have been investigations, like Janet Reno's, but I believe that the illegal actions of the police have either been whitewashed or covered up.

The following incident is a perfect example of illegal activity that continued the entire ten years of the lawsuit. Years before the Nancy situation, an insider in the police department informed me that the police were illegally tapping my phone. I called the phone company to check our lines. The representative from BellSouth said that one of the wires to our phone was on top of a tangle of wires located in a phone box right behind the building where police did their undercover work.

I told Wayne that it was time to catch the police in action. To accomplish this, I would call a friend of mine in the black community who was in on our plan.

"I have some really interesting information about the police department, but I don't want to tell you over the phone. I'll be right there," I told her in a conspiratorial manner."

I got into my car and immediately left for my friend's home. Wayne had been alerted to follow when he saw a police car pulling out behind me. The policeman circled the block after I went into my friend's home and then parked behind a fence next to the house.

Wayne recognized the driver and pulled up right next to him. "Hey, Bob, what are you doing here?" he asked with an I-already-know-what-you-are-doing-here tone of voice.

Bob looked like he was shocked to see Wayne. He became very flustered, made some silly excuse, and left.

Of course, I immediately made a formal complaint to the police department, which was never acknowledged. As far as I know, the police continued tapping my phone without a warrant long after I retired.

CITY OF DELRAY BEACH

100 N.W. 1st AVENUE · DELRAY BEACH, FLORIDA 33444 · 407/243-7000

DEC 4 2000

November 30, 2000

1993

Mrs. Virginia Snyder
38 S. Swinton Avenue
Delray Beach, FL 33444

Dear Mrs. Snyder:

This letter is sent in the spirit of reconciliation. You are a valued, long-standing resident of the City of Delray Beach. We appreciate your contributions to the City.

Unfortunately, this long-lasting dispute has, over the past eleven years, placed us in an adversarial position. The City Commission believes that it is in all the parties' best interests to end the dispute so that we can go forward together in harmony to address issues currently facing the City.

In the spirit of compromise, the City acknowledges that it acted through its employees. The City believed and still believes that its employees were acting in good faith. Our officers were attempting to correct what they perceived to be actual threats to officer safety by virtue of information leaked from the Police Department. Our investigation concluded, however, that you, Virginia Snyder, violated no Florida Statutes, nor were you involved in any criminal activity in any way.

The City Commission sincerely hopes that you accept the sentiments expressed in this letter of reconciliation.

Sincerely,

David W. Schmidt
Mayor

Printed on Recycled Paper

THE EFFORT ALWAYS MATTERS

THE DIAZ CASE AND JANET RENO

I was determined to bring justice to Luis Diaz. On March 23, 1990, I sent Reno a letter that began: "Today is Luis Diaz' 52nd birthday. He has been in prison since 1979 for crimes he didn't do; I am appealing to you to correct this injustice."

I specified important new evidence I had uncovered, and the letter ended with, "I know how busy you must be, but I know also that you are a fair and responsible prosecutor and have faith in you to take whatever measures are necessary to right this terrible wrong."

Reno responded on July 27, 1990: "Upon receipt of your letter … I asked Don Horn to review the whole case anew…. He had no previous contact with the Diaz case. He has advised me that he does not see a basis for setting aside the jury's verdict."

When I gave Luis's son and daughter-in-law, Jose and Ileana, the bad news, they wrote to Janet Reno. I wrote again. Janet Reno then wrote to Roy Black, Diaz's original attorney, and told him that she would "be happy to discuss any type of investigation or follow-up he suggests."

Black responded to her on August 27, 1990, explaining that he had not worked on the case since the first trial and that Diaz "was represented by other counsel on his appeals. Accordingly, I presently have no authority to represent him in any of the matters that have been discussed between you and Virginia Snyder."

Reno responded on January 8, 1991, with another letter to Roy Black: "This is to confirm and reiterate the position set forth over the past year (letters to Ms. Snyder of July 27, and August 9, and 23; letter to you of August 31; and letter to Mr. And Mrs. Diaz of August 10,

1990) that I will be happy to discuss with you any type of investigation or follow-up you think this office should undertake in this case."

I began to feel as if I were in the twilight zone. Why did Janet Reno insist on following up on Diaz's case with Roy Black, who wrote and explained to her that he no longer had any authority to represent Diaz? Why had no one interviewed Luis Nunez about his affidavit? I decided to try again and wrote a long letter to Reno on March 26, 1991, specifying all the new information I had uncovered that warranted a new trial for Luis. The following is the entire content of the letter:

Dear Ms. Reno:

Once again, I'm appealing to you on behalf of Mr. Diaz. I know Mr. Horn reviewed the file and found no reason to reopen the case. However, I feel that, had witnesses been questioned and information followed up on that was not available at the time of trial, he would have reached a different conclusion.

In the beginning, Fred Mendez, a Spanish-speaking police officer, completely fabricated interviews with witnesses, thus getting enough 'evidence' for a Probable Cause Affidavit. Mendez was later charged with five counts of falsifying reports in other cases. This is new information.

Jesse Patmore, the Anglo officer who accompanied Mendez on his interviews with the Spanish-speaking 'witnesses,' quit the force before the Diaz trial and moved to North Carolina. He was never called as a witness.

I feel sure Patmore knew the interviewees were not giving statements to Mendez. It isn't necessary to know the language to recognize when a witness is saying he or she doesn't know anything. Patmore returned to the force, after the trial. This is new information.

Police showed victims photo lineups, then live lineups, then video tapes of the live lineups, sometimes more than once, before the victims 'recognized' Diaz.

120

At least one victim was still unsure if Diaz was her attacker, even up to just before she testified, according to another victim with whom she was talking in the corridor. <u>This is new information.</u>

Another victim told me, after the trial, that she had made a mistake when she identified Diaz and testified against him. She said she knew she had made a mistake when the same car followed her after Diaz was in prison. <u>This is new information.</u>

Years after the trial, when I contacted another victim, she asked if I could send her photos of Diaz without a shirt on. I did so but she never told me what she was looking for. This was after I had sent her a copy of a photo of the man I believe to be the leader of the gang of rapists, Juan Delatoree, along with a photo of another member of his gang and a mug shot of Diaz. <u>This is new information.</u>

Lou Altobellie, who was a PSD officer at the time of the rapes and who investigated them, told me after the trial that he had looked at one of their own officers but would not tell me who it was. He did, however, predict that, if I solved the rapes, I would find at least one, and possibly two, officers were involved. <u>This is new information.</u>

Atobellie was pulled off the case and told not to continue his investigation.

A member of Delatorre's gang, Luis Nunez, signed an Affidavit that the gang committed the rapes. <u>This is new information.</u> Nunez did not participate in the rapes, only in the robberies, drug-related crimes, etc., he told me, because he had little girls.

Doug LeCroy, of Miami, now on Death Row, gave me information about the rapes and did not involve Diaz. I worked with LeCroy's defense attorney when he was tried for murder in Palm Beach County. <u>This is new information.</u>

There are a number of friends and associates or others who have information about Delatorre who could be questioned, as well as people associated with his cousin, Armando Alonso, the gang member most likely to 'talk,' according to Nunez.

Diaz has been polygraphed by a bi-lingual polygraphist who has cleared him of any involvement in the rapes. <u>This is new information.</u>

Diaz is not in prison because he committed any crime. <u>He is in prison because of crooked cops who framed him,</u> then lied in court.

Diaz's son has a home and a job waiting for his father when he is free.

Diaz just had his 53rd birthday and has spent the last 12 years of his life in Florida's crudest, toughest maximum security prison. He has lost the home he worked so hard to buy. He has lost his wife who believed in his innocence but finally came to believe that he would never be released from prison. He has lost the precious years of seeing his three children grow to adulthood.

In the interest of justice, Ms. Reno, I am pleading with you to reopen this case. Please let Mary Cagle [an assistant district attorney] read the seven file folders I sent to you. Your office has the authority to question, to check records, to grant immunity or plea bargain with witnesses/defendants.

Finally, Roy Black has agreed to represent Diaz, pro bono, if he is given a new trial. Thank you for listening. I have faith that you will do what is in the best interest of justice.

Sincerely,

I received a call three weeks later from Ray Haven, chief investigator for Janet Reno's office. However, the tone of his voice and the direction of his conversation left no doubt in my mind that he was just going through the motions and that any investigation he did would be to confirm that Diaz was guilty. The one positive statement that Haven made to me about his investigation was that he believed that more than one person was involved in the Bird Road rapes, because of the different descriptions of the witnesses. However, he intended to report to Reno that the case be closed.

If he believed that there were other rapists involved, why would he not reopen the case to look for them? I was too busy holding in my anger to actually ask him that question, but I did remind Haven that there was never, at any time, any evidence or testimony that Diaz had friends, co-workers, or associates who could be the other rapists. He did not answer this comment.

After reading Havens's report to Janet Reno, I sent another letter to her: "Haven's arrogance and insulting attitude when he spoke to me in April was only exceeded by his incompetent and unprofessional approach to this investigation." Then I specified the reasons for this statement. I ended the letter with, "I will continue to try to get [Diaz] out of prison."

I had spent years in a futile attempt to get Reno to open the case. Then I decided to go public and contacted the television program *Unsolved Mysteries*. The producers did a half-hour show, during which they interviewed Luis Nunez. He told the audience all of the same information he gave me in his sworn affidavit. The show was taped in December of 1992 and was aired in March of 1993.

Almost immediately, Janet Reno assigned another assistant attorney, Kevin DiGregory, to review the case. He finally interviewed Donna Coppage, who had recanted her identification of Diaz as her attacker ten years earlier and who had never been interviewed by anyone in Reno's office. One of the first questions he asked her was whether Virginia Snyder had told her what to say about Diaz and whether Roy Black had talked to her. Indeed, when I spoke to Donna after the interview, she told me that she had the distinct impression that DiGregory had doubts about my professional ability and competence, at which time I had the distinct feeling of déjá-vu.

My overwhelming frustration increased when I learned that DiGregory had not bothered to interview Luis Nunez. Nunez died in prison in December of 1994, never having been contacted by anyone in Reno's office. Not surprisingly, the other rapists have never been brought to justice.

There is an interesting footnote to the whole Reno saga. When she was being considered as a nominee for the post of attorney general, I received a call from President Clinton's office. The head of the vetting team asked me about Reno.

"First, tell me how you got my name," I requested, surprised to receive such a call.

"Janet gave it to us when we asked her if there was anyone who would have anything negative to say about her," the caller explained.

I told the member of the vetting team that I admired Reno as a person because she was honest and extremely bright. However, I did not admire her as a district attorney because her judgment about those people she trusted and listened to was wanting. I commented that I would support another woman who was then on the Florida Supreme Court.

"We're vetting her, too," the caller stated.

My nominee was later appointed to a federal judgeship, but Janet Reno served as the first female U.S. attorney general during both of Clinton's terms, 1993–2001.

Four years later, about a week after Luis was declared a free man, Janet Reno was quoted in *The Miami Herald*, in an article about my role in the Diaz case: "Reno said this week that at the time, Snyder could be 'very difficult to deal with.… She was not as objective as she could be in presenting her positions. If she'd been more objective, she'd have been more effective.'"[1]

Now I do not know what to think about Janet Reno.

---

[1] Elinor J. Brecher, "Wrong Righted, Sleuth Can Now Rest Easy at 84," The Miami Herald, August 11, 2005.

THE FREE MILLIE CASE

The next and very memorable case began with a phone call in June of 1993. The caller sounded desperate.

"My friend, Millie Reeves, is being held prisoner in her own home, cut off from all of her friends. I've tried everything to get help for her, but I can't. Can you help?"

"How did you get my name?" I asked.

"I called the American Civil Liberties Union, and the woman in charge referred me to you. She said that it would take time for their agency to investigate, but you could get on it right away. You've got to help me," he pleaded.

That was the beginning of our "Free Millie Case." Millie Reeves was a lively widow who lived two doors away from the Kennedy compound in Palm Beach. Years earlier, she and Rose Kennedy went for walks together in the lush, quiet neighborhoods. Millie also loved to go to parties. Palm Beachers remember her for her shocking red hair, fancy outfits, and flamboyant hats. Photos of her at various social functions appeared regularly in the *Palm Beach Daily News*. In fact, most of her wardrobe consisted of party dresses! Millie loved to dance, but she also loved to use her brain. At the age of eighty-eight, she still read newspapers and magazines and was known for her witty conversation.

The caller that June day was Jack Sullivan, whose mother had been a friend to Millie. Jack had known Millie for over two decades. When he learned that she had recently returned from a nursing home, he bought flowers and went to visit her. He was shocked when he was told that he was not allowed to see Millie or leave the flowers.

"A caregiver ordered me to leave, saying that I was not on a list of people the guardian had given to the police. When I insisted on seeing Millie, the caregiver called the police. They threatened to arrest me if I didn't leave!"

Jack went on to explain that Millie's quality of life had begun to decline a year earlier when she fell out of bed and injured her hip. After a stay in the hospital, she was transferred to a nursing home for rehabilitation. While she was there, the Department of Health and Rehabilitative Services concluded that Millie was unable to care for herself physically and that she displayed irrational behavior. Following an evaluation by two psychiatrists, a judge ruled that she was incapacitated. Millie had no living relatives, and Stanley Hyman, forty-seven and a West Palm Beach attorney, won guardianship of her and her property in December of 1992.

Jack told me that her friends insisted that Millie was alert during her rehabilitation, reading newspapers and magazines, watching news on TV, and discussing the upcoming elections. They thought that Millie was probably done in by her habit of lying about her age. She still insisted that she was in her late forties! There was also evidence that she had even doctored a document or two.

"But if everyone in Palm Beach who lied about their age was declared incompetent, the whole town would be in trouble," a neighbor pointed out.

One of the psychiatrists who examined Millie called her a "romanticist," a trait that "linked with delusional thinking hinders her ability to be rational about some of life's issues," according to his report. Jack believed that Millie's civil rights were being violated and wanted me to investigate.

I immediately contacted Millie's neighbors across the street, Charles and June Shepherd, and told them what Jack had told me. They had been out of town for the previous six months and had no knowledge about what was happening to Millie. I arranged to pay a surprise visit to Millie with them on the following Sunday. I would pose as a friend of theirs.

The caregiver, obviously rattled by the unexpected visit, checked the list of restricted people. Charles and June were not on it, perhaps because they had been out of town. She reluctantly let us in. Millie was lying on a sofa, dressed in a long T-shirt.

"You remember June, don't you, Millie?" Charles asked.

Millie nodded, smiled politely, and held out her hand. She began to reminisce about their daughter's wedding.

Before we went to Millie's house, I had asked her friends to talk about as many subjects as possible, so that we could evaluate Millie's mental condition. They carried on a very careful conversation with Millie, aware that the caregiver was listening to everything. Although Millie was very frail physically, she was alert mentally. As she and the Shepherds talked about events and friends, there was never any indication that she was the least bit confused.

Under the pretext that I needed to call my husband, I asked to use the phone and confirmed what Jack had told me: no outgoing calls could be made on that line.

"We have another phone for necessary calls," the aide said when I asked what would happen if Millie had an emergency.

Our visit confirmed Jack's fears. When I returned home and dialed Millie's number, I also confirmed Jack's concern that all phone calls to Millie were being forwarded to Hyman's office. I began a thorough check on Hyman and all other aspects of the case. Reading the court file, I learned that the circuit judge handling guardianship cases in the South County division in Delray Beach was Michael F. Gersten, said to be a friend of Hyman's. The original circuit judge assigned to the case was in the main courthouse in West Palm Beach. Hyman petitioned for a change of venue to South County in Delray Beach, where Gersten would supervise him. The change of venue was granted, even though West Palm Beach would have been a much better location for the guardianship, because all of Millie's property was in Palm Beach, and Hyman's longtime office was in West Palm Beach.

Gersten denied showing any favoritism to Hyman, but the judge largely ignored Hyman's guardianship reports or else did not read them at all. These reports actually detailed Hyman's cruel actions toward Millie, which should have alerted Gersten to investigate Hyman. For example, Millie was punished for disobeying any one of the six-page long list of house rules. Hyman himself reported that he took Millie's walker away because she had gained access to a caregiver's phone and called a friend. Her beloved shih tzu, Lover Boy, was taken to a kennel for a week as punishment for another infraction. Hyman's reports also stated that he boarded up her bedroom window after she tried to call for help and put a lock on her bedroom door to prevent her from getting out. He even put locks on the refrigerator to prevent her from retrieving food for the dog! He charged for his time in doing all of this of course—at one hundred dollars an hour.

On July 6, 1993, I wrote a twelve-page letter to Judge Gersten, imploring him to investigate the guardianship. On July 9, Gersten issued an order to Hyman that he should respond to my allegations within thirty days. Hyman responded in a letter that Millie had no access to the phone because "all she is doing is getting herself all worked up about what she perceives as my misappropriation of her treasures. The screening of her calls through my office is necessary to weed out the panderers." He described Millie as a difficult ward, verbally abusive, destructive to the furniture, and unrepentant when she was found hiding food for her dog, even though the dog was well fed.

Indeed, Millie complained about "misappropriations of her treasures."

Hyman had kept Millie in the nursing home way past the time for her release. Millie would ask her physician when she would be going home, and he would tell her to ask her guardian, because medically there was no reason to keep her. When she finally did get home, she found that virtually all of her possessions were missing.

"It was like walking into a stranger's house," Millie told me later.

Her jewelry, dresses, hats, purses, shoes, and a full-length chinchilla coat and matching hat were gone. Even her late husband's ashes and those of her previous dog had vanished! (Both had been in sterling silver containers.) All of her numerous photos, showing her with well-known Palm Beachers and famous visitors—many in sterling silver frames—were gone. Her bookcases, which had been filled with books, were empty. Not surprisingly, there was no sign of her expensive china and sterling silver flatware. There was even missing furniture. Hyman explained Millie's missing clothes and furniture by saying that they were all badly soiled and he had to have them removed. A longtime friend of Millie was outraged that all the ball gowns were gone.

"Even if they were soiled, they could have been cleaned," she said. "Those gowns belonged in a museum."

A witness I found had seen Hyman's female employees sorting Millie's things and putting them in separate piles. That same witness saw someone break up Millie's antique secretary and throw it into the dumpster. Millie had kept all her jewelry in that secretary.

Thirty-six people had tried to contact Millie in the last three months through letters, phone calls, cards, and visits. No one was successful. Also, anything sent to the house—candy, flowers—was sent back. Hyman later contended that he kept people away because they were exploiting Millie.

I was able to use a party for Millie's eighty-ninth birthday to let her know surreptitiously that help was on the way. I had learned about a man who was an acquaintance of Hyman and who was allowed access to Millie. Hyman probably wanted someone to pretend he had an interest in Millie so she had someone to talk to and hopefully to confide in. I managed to become friendly with this man, pretending that I was an old school acquaintance of Millie who had not seen her for years. He told me that he had invited some of his friends to a small birthday party for Millie at his house. I could also come. I pretended to be very excited to see Millie after so many years and got permission to bring a friend.

The night of the party, the man picked up Millie and brought her to his house. My friend, who was actually a *Palm Beach Post* reporter, arrived shortly after I did. We were both introduced by the fake names we were using and settled into the party. Millie was dressed in a pink gown and wore lots of make-up. Guests hugged and kissed her, as one would expect on such an occasion. I managed to sit next to her at one point. In a low voice, I told Millie that I was a private eye, that we were going to free her as soon as we could, and that the tall man standing near the window was a reporter.

Her reaction was perfect, very low key, like "That's nice." However, I could tell from her body language that she knew what was going on and was playing along. I am certain that she recognized me from the visit with her neighbors, Charles and June. There was nothing wrong with Millie's mind, and I was more determined than ever to set her free.

A short time later, I decided to write to Chief Judge Jack Cook, because Gersten was not doing his job of protecting Millie. Only then did Gersten appoint Ronald Perry, a social worker with experience as a guardian, to monitor the guardianship and present a full report by September 10, 1993. This was still not enough for Jack Sullivan, who was now fully alarmed about Millie's situation. He retained attorney

Stuart Klein to take legal action to protect Millie and get Hyman removed as guardian. Klein petitioned the court on Jack's behalf to appoint Jack as guardian.

On September 9, one day before the social worker's final report was due, Hyman resigned. Millie was finally free after ten months! As it turned out, Perry recommended in his report that Millie should have a different guardian, because Hyman had gone too far with his control. "A true spirit of least restrictive mentality should be here," he wrote. On September 13, Jack was appointed guardian of Millie's person, and a bank was appointed guardian of her property.

Millie spent the next two years in comfort. Jack moved in with her, furnishing her house with beautiful antiques he bought. (Her own resources had been depleted under Hyman's guardianship, and no one thought that a lengthy lawsuit would be productive at her age.) Jack also took her—in a wheelchair—to luncheons and balls, where she looked happy and beautiful in gowns he purchased from chic consignment shops. Millie was very grateful that Jack had come to her rescue and appreciated every day of those last two years. She died on April 4, 1996, at the age of ninety-one.

Millie was gone but not forgotten. I kept track of Hyman after she died. At first, it appeared that he would get away with his crime against her, because we were not able to have him charged with anything in Millie's case. However, he was arrested on September 6, 2001, for allegedly robbing twelve other wards. He was charged with twenty-four counts of racketeering, an organized scheme to defraud his wards of over fifty thousand dollars, exploitation of an elderly or disabled person, and grand theft.

On May 11, 2005, after four years, Hyman was allowed to plead guilty to defrauding seniors, but he did not get any jail time. Instead, he was sentenced to ten years probation, agreed to forfeit his law license, and agreed to pay forty-eight thousand dollars in restitution to five victims. However, his probation may be terminated after five years if he pays the restitution and meets other conditions.

"The mills of the gods grind slowly …"

WE SAY GOOD-BYE
TO SHOJI

In 1990, Shoji came home when I received the Susan B. Anthony Award from the South County Chapter of NOW. He was in excellent spirits and seemed to be in good health. However, on his next visit that year, I sensed that there was something wrong. He had lost weight and looked haggard; his clothes hung on him as though they belonged to someone else. Ross and I urged him to see a doctor. Then he told us that he had been seeing doctors off and on, but that they did not know what was wrong with him. Hatsue assured us that she and Shoji would take care of his health.

We were very worried, but Shoji assured us that he was able to get along. Over the next six years, he continued to look thin and drawn and to see various specialists. No doctor had a diagnosis, but Shoji said that at least he was not getting worse. We chose to believe him.

We should have been suspicious when he was not able to get home for my seventy-sixth birthday in November of 1996. He wrote: "To most people, November is a reminder that winter and Christmas are on the way, but to me it means the month that holds the birthday of my mother. I certainly miss you, particularly at this time of the year. Near or far, Mom, on your birthday as on every day, I am thinking of you with love and affection." And I missed him.

When Shoji came home six months later, for Ross's seventy-sixth birthday, we were shocked by his appearance. The term "skin and bones" is the only way I can describe him. He was very weak and had trouble walking. He returned a few months later and could not even stand up! We were absolutely stunned to see how fast his health had deteriorated. The doctors were still puzzled about his illness.

Shoji had lost all hope and told us that he had planned to commit suicide in Japan but decided that he would rather come home to die near us. We were heartbroken.

After a few days, Shoji insisted on going to a motel, the Bermuda Inn on the beach in Delray Beach. We begged him to stay with us, but he was adamant about not dying in our home. He had stopped eating solid food and would take only liquids. We made sure that he had a constant source of whatever he wanted to drink and stayed with him as much as he would allow,

In the middle of the afternoon on September 18, 1997, he asked us to take him to the hospital. I called an ambulance. I rode in front with the driver, because I was not allowed to ride in the back. Ross followed us in the car.

The doctors in the emergency room asked us if we wanted to take any extraordinary measures to keep him alive. We knew that he wanted to die and said no. The staff was very understanding. We were allowed to stay by his side for three hours until he died. Hatsue was still in Japan, because he did not want her to see him die.

I was standing at the head of his bed, stroking his face and hair, when he looked at me and whispered, "I'm dying." He closed his eyes. The doctor pronounced him dead. Shoji was only fifty-one. How tragic for this wonderful man to have died so young! However, our devastating sadness was also tempered with relief for the end of Shoji's suffering.

When we saw the death certificate, it read, "Cause of death pending." What horrible illness had plagued our Shoji the last seven or eight years of his life? Not until after the autopsy did we learn that Shoji died of spinocerebellar degeneration, a congenital form of progressive dysfunction of the cerebellum, spinal cord, and peripheral nerves, for which there is no cure. Somehow, it made it easier to realize that no one or nothing could have helped our Shoji. It took a while, but we were able to make peace with his death.

Shoji was cremated, according to his wishes, and we gave half of his ashes to his brother and Hatsue, who arrived shortly after his death. The other half we placed in our garden and planted an atemoya tree in his memory. In November of 1997, we had a memorial service in his honor, to which we invited old friends from the VTA days and new friends from his Shoji Snyder days. He had been our son for twenty-three years, and we were very grateful.

I agree with Alfred Lord Tennyson: "'Tis better to have loved and lost/Than never to have loved at all."

Shoji's Ashes

Muscles that once were strong, wasting away,
His body getting weaker day by day.
No longer in charge of his life or death,
Or when he would take his final breath,
He looked up at me with eyes opened wide,
"I'm dying," he said softly.
Then he died.

The atemoya tree is growing tall.
It doesn't seem like any time at all
Since friends and loved ones placed his ashes there
And planted the small sapling with great care.
How happy he would be to watch it grow.
But there is one thing we will never know:
Is he content with resting down below,
Or would he choose to feel the breezes blow?
I like to think that once the lights are out,
His soul slips up to have a look about.

THE DIAZ CASE:
THE INNOCENCE
PROJECT

One very positive effect of the 1993 *Unsolved Mysteries* program for Luis Diaz was that another victim, besides Donna Coppage, recanted her testimony against Diaz. Based on this, Diaz's lawyers filed a motion in 1994 to have his conviction overturned. Seven years later, in 2001, prosecutors vacated the convictions involving the two witnesses who had recanted. Thus, Luis became eligible for parole.

I was thrilled at the possibility of Luis's being freed, even if the remaining five convictions stood. To our great disappointment, however, parole was denied in 2003. I was now more worried than ever that Luis would spend the rest of his life in prison, because parole boards rarely release sex offenders when so many accusers are involved.

Fortunately, Jose Diaz had been pursuing another tactic. In 1998, he read an article about the Innocence Project and decided that he would write to this organization about his father. I wholeheartedly agreed. The Innocence Project is a non-profit clinic that handles only those cases where DNA testing of evidence can result in definite proof of innocence for people in prison, like Luis Diaz. Started in 1992 by nationally known civil rights attorneys Barry C. Scheck and Peter J. Neufeld, the Project focuses on wrongful convictions.

Under the supervision of the Innocence Project staff attorneys and co-directors, law school students at numerous law schools across the country assist with fact development and investigations, particularly biological evidence. For example, the Florida Innocence Project at Nova Southeastern University Law Center in Davie, Florida, and the Florida

135

Innocence Project Initiative at the Florida State University School of Law in Tallahassee, Florida, are both offshoots of the original Innocence Project founded by Barry Scheck and Peter Neufeld.

The Innocence Project gets as many as two hundred new requests a month. As a result, even though Jose sent his letter in 1998, he did not receive a reply until September of 2003, the same year we thought all hope was lost because Luis had been denied parole. We were elated to learn that the Innocence Project would take Luis's case. In true roller coaster fashion, we were also very apprehensive, because Luis's lawyers faced a deadline for filing applications based on DNA evidence, which was only one month away. A cooperative effort between Barry Scheck of the Innocence Project, the staff of the Florida Initiative, and lawyers in the Florida office of Holland and Knight got the job done.

From all the evidence at Luis's trial, only one rape kit remained, that of one of the witnesses who recanted. At least there was one! Prosecutors agreed to test the rape kit, which was sent to SERI in California. In the meantime, evidence from the same rape kit was sent to the Miami Dade Police Department Crime Laboratory for testing. In June of 2005, results from both laboratories proved Luis innocent of the rape. I knew it.

Now prosecutors were interested in looking at evidence in all cases attributed to the Bird Road Rapist, not just the evidence from victims who testified against Luis. One other rape kit was also found. As soon as I heard about the second rape kit, I began celebrating. I knew that Luis would be exonerated.

The evidence was sent to the Miami Dade Police Department Crime Laboratory. Again, results proved that Luis was not the contributor of the semen. Even better, the results showed the DNA of this second kit matched that of the first. In other words, the same man raped both victims.

It was now the fall of 2004 and time to begin my annual Christmas letter. I wrote of the positive developments in Luis's case, including his soon-to-be exoneration. Even though I was certain that Luis would be freed, I decided to wait until the event to mail the letters. In the meantime, the tireless Barry Scheck was negotiating day after day with the prosecutors to have all counts against Luis dropped. This would take a year.

Colin Starger, one of the other lawyers at the Innocence Project, told me later that all of the new evidence I had found in the twenty-six years helped to convince the prosecutors to exonerate Luis of all charges. We did not know until the last minute, the morning of August 3, 2005, that this would happen and that Louis would be released.

THE DIAZ CASE: LUIS'S LAST DAY IN COURT

The day had dawned bright and clear, like most other days in Florida; but it was not like other days. Luis Diaz would be walking out of prison, and I would be there to see it. Even though I was eighty-five and had long avoided driving on I-95, I was prepared to make the long drive to the Dade County Courthouse myself. (Ross had not been driving for a few years.) Nothing was going to keep me away from the courthouse that morning! But my nephew Wayne knew how much this meant to me, and he was also eager to be there, so he drove Ross and me there.

We arrived early, but the Diaz family was already there. Caridad and the children welcomed me with hugs and kisses, while making room for Ross and me to sit with them. After so many years of false hopes and frustration, I could not believe that Luis was actually going to be set free. I expected to feel very excited; instead, I felt totally numb as we waited for Luis to appear in the courtroom. State officials needed time to bring him from the prison to the jail and now to the courthouse. So we waited.

Then Luis entered the courtroom and threw a kiss in our direction. Suddenly, I was caught up in the joyful anticipation exhibited by his family. I finally realized that it was real; Luis was going to be free! I grabbed Ross's hand and squeezed it. I hugged Jose and then Luis's older brother, Antonio, and all of the members of the family I could reach. Now it began to seem like a celebration. The judge liberated Luis at 11:52 a.m. Still, we needed to wait until the paperwork was all completed before we could see Luis walk out of the courthouse a free man. The excitement was building. His family had bought new street clothes for him to wear.

When Luis walked through the door, he was wearing a new *guayabere*, new trousers, and new shoes. Caridad had made the purchases for him. Antonio had brought a cup of Cuban coffee for him to drink as soon as he stepped through the door. The smile on Luis's face, a smile of pure happiness, caught at our hearts. I felt tears well up in my eyes as he hugged the members of his family who crowded around him. His love for Caridad was warmly received, and I remember thinking and hoping that maybe they would become one family again.

As he hugged me, I thanked whatever gods may be that I had lived long enough to see this day. The next morning, I finally mailed my Christmas letters.

Two days after learning the results of the DNA test, Governor Jeb Bush issued an executive order that no police department was to destroy DNA evidence, no matter how old. What a wonderful and well-deserved tribute to Barry Scheck and the Innocence Project!

However, this comes way too late to help Luis get monetary compensation for all those years he was wrongfully imprisoned. Although Luis was exonerated of the other five crimes for which he was convicted, he has not been proven innocent of those crimes, because there is no DNA evidence available for those cases. I am hopeful that something can be worked out between the family and the state of Florida so that Luis can receive proper compensation for twenty-six years of living in the toughest prison in South Florida.

Luis is now living with his daughter, Marilyn, her husband, Dan, and their two children. Luis shares a bedroom with his eleven-year-old grandson at the time of this writing, but Marilyn and Dan are hoping to add another bedroom and bathroom onto their home for him. His former wife, Caridad, is often with him and the children. I keep expecting an announcement that she and Luis will remarry.

One of the strangest aspects of the Diaz case is that eight witnesses were wrong in identifying him as their attacker. In fact, Barry Scheck said that the previous record of witnesses identifying the wrong man was five, so the Diaz case was a landmark for reforms in using police photo and live lineups.

At present, police departments use mostly photo lineups. Witnesses are supervised by the detectives on the case who know who the suspect is. These detectives show the victim six mug shots of people, all at one time. As Lisa Arthur and Jay Weaver wrote in the *Miami Herald*, ("Police Lineup Methods Flawed" 8/4/05), " Researchers say that when witnesses are shown all six photos at once—rather than one at a time—a natural tendency kicks in to compare faces and judge which looks most like the one they remember. They make a relative judgment as opposed to a true recognition, experts say."

Also, when the detective showing the photos knows the suspect, that information is often translated to the witness by body language. These detectives are often not even aware of their demeanor.

Reformers believe that photos should be shown one at a time; either the witness recognizes that one or he/she does not. Equally as important, the detective supervising the photo lineup should not be on the case.

In the same Arthur and Weaver article, Barry Scheck explained that of the 160 exonerations resulting from the Innocence Project, "120 involved mistaken witness identifications.... This reform movement has reached a tipping point, and I strongly feel the Diaz case is going to push it over the top."

I agree that reforms are needed. If the Diaz case can hasten them along, then perhaps Luis's sacrifice was not in vain.

Happy Birthday, Luis

Happy Birthday, Luis. Heaven's sake, you've waited long. Twenty-six years have passed without a birthday song.

Now that you're sixty-eight, now that you're finally free, I'm sending you all my love—HAPPY BIRTHDAY FROM ME!

March 15, 2006

CONCLUSION

It's so much easier to grow old when you've done something with your life.
—Bernice "Gee" Hayden, WASP pilot, WWII

In 1982, after I appeared on the NBC show *Today*, the network's vice president for program development contacted me to do a series about Virginia Snyder, Private Eye, based on my life as a little old lady who lives in the oldest residence in Delray Beach, who specializes in murder cases, and who is also a writer. Later, NBC decided to drop the idea, and the vice president for program development, who had originally approached me but who now worked for CBS, asked his new bosses if they were interested in the series about me.

They declined, but about a year later, CBS had a new series about Jessica Fletcher as the little old private eye, specializing in murder cases. She lived in the oldest house in Cabot Cove and was also a writer. My attorney said that I could sue, because I had documentation of my initial contact with NBC and of our approach to CBS. However, I knew that such a lawsuit would tie me up completely and disrupt all of my work as a private investigator. I did not care about the money; we were frugal and had everything we needed. I decided not to sue and have never regretted it.

A short while after I retired in 1999, I self-published *Poems of Fact and Fantasy,* a compilation of one hundred poems I wrote over a fifty-year period, from the ages of eighteen to sixty-eight. That was how I met Sandra Sobel Reddemann. She was teaching my grandniece Nicole at the time. When Nicole showed her my book, Mrs. Reddemann invited me to talk to her class about poetry. That was how we established the friendship that led to our co-authoring *… And Justice For All,* one of the most important events in my retirement.

I still hear from former clients I helped over the years. Phone calls and letters about their gratitude and successes often bring tears of joy to my eyes. Mark Herman came from Arizona to see me in 2007. I am very proud of all the work I did to help people find their way out of the labyrinth that is our judicial system. My concern was always about making a difference, never about making a lot of money. I did everything I could to help people, and I am satisfied, not besieged by "could haves," "should haves," or "would haves."

My life is much quieter now. Nine years ago, Ross was diagnosed with Alzheimer's disease. I am now his caregiver, and Ross's well being is foremost in my life. He is still my sweet, loving husband, although his recognition of his surroundings has narrowed significantly. For example, he tells me that I am his "loving wife" whenever I ask him who I am, but he no longer knows where or what the refrigerator is. We take each day as it comes, and I will be here for him, no matter what. Every day I hope that I will hear about new medication for his condition. After all, I know what it is to wait—and wait—for good news and to keep hoping for the best.

It is March 13, 2007, and I have just lost (and won) the election for mayor of Delray Beach. I expected to lose the vote when I decided to run the previous December.

That is when I was approached by the leadership of Save Delray, an organization founded for the purpose of slowing down the burgeoning development in our city. The group wanted someone to oppose the only candidate running for mayor of Delray Beach, because she was vice mayor of the City Commission and past president of the Chamber of Commerce during the unbridled residential and commercial development of recent years. We also believed that our city government needed to address the rising crime and gang-related violence that was facing all of Palm Beach County.

Neither issue was stressed on this candidate's platform. In fact, my soon-to-be opponent favored big developers and seemed to ignore the crime problems. I was in a unique position: despite my eighty-six years, I had the energy and the money to take on the race for mayor. My only purpose was to raise the ignored issues before the general voting public.

It was a hectic few months of meetings and interviews and more interviews. Fortunately, Ross's two daughters had recently moved to

West Palm Beach and were available to stay with him when I went to evening meetings. My campaign manager, Diane Heinz, took every opportunity to present our issues and me to the public. Gradually, the opposition, and what I consider to be the establishment, altered its platform to address our issues, promising responsible development and attention to rising crime problems.

I received 28 percent of the vote, so I lost. However, we changed the dialogue of the election, so we won. Now I plan to attend as many meetings as I can to hold the mayor to her promises. I'm still ready for a challenge, and I'm only eighty-six years young!

Wedding photo of W. F. "Frank" and Leota M. Dean,
February 2, 1917

Virginia Alice Artip, age 3 years

Virginia, age 9 years

Virginia, ninth grade

Rev. B. F. And Lillian Connerly

Virginia with her first husband, Hendrix Royston, 1949

Virginia with her second husband, Ross Snyder, 1953

Virginia and U. S. Congressman Paul G. Rogers,
keynote speaker at the National Mental Association convention
where Virginia received the Bell Award, Nov. 21, 1974

1984

REWARD

$3,000 in CASH
&
A new Buick

Jimmy Shepherd, age 16

FOR ANY INFORMATION
LEADING TO THE ARREST
AND CONVICTION IN THE
MURDER OF JIMMY SHEPHERD
(His body was found in Delray in June 1982)

Please Contact:
Virginia Snyder,
Private Investigator

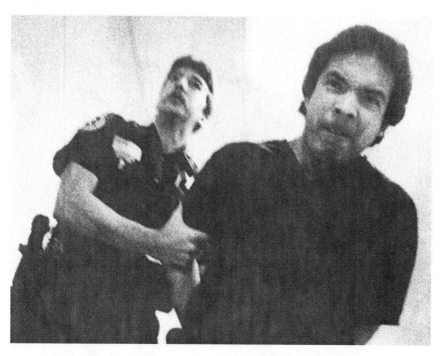

Omar Galvez in police custody, May, 1990

Virginia and Ross when they retired
December, 1998

Virginia with Millie Reeves, 1993

Virginia and Ross with Shoji, 1982

Shoji with a friend, 1997

Luis Diaz, 67, on the day of his release
(printed in *The New Youk Times,* August 3, 2005)

Luis Diaz, Jose Diaz, the oldest son, and Virginia, shortly after
Luis' Release August, 2005

Virginia, 2007

Luis Ciaz in the 1970's with his wife, Caridad and their children, from left, Jose, Marilyn, and Alberto. (printed in *The New Youk Times,* August 3, 2005)

Printed in the United States
124386LV00002B/391-549/P

9 780595 450763